INDIAN VISTAS OF ENVIRONMENT

INDIAN VISTAS OF ENVIRONMENT

Editors

CHITTABRATA PALIT

MAHUA SARKAR

PUBLICATIONS

KALPAZ PUBLICATIONS

DELHI-110052

Indian Vistas of Environment

Rs. 590

ISBN: 81-7855-596-5

Published in 2007 in India by
Kalpaz Publications
C-30, Satyawati Nagar,
Delhi-110052
E-mail: kalpaz@hotmail.com

Laser Type Setting by: Rudra Computer Graphics, Delhi
Printed at : Salasar Imaging System, Delhi

Contents

Preface

This book has grown out of a refresher course on environment at the History Department of Jadavpur University. We wish to thank the Head and the staff of the Department for facilitating the course and the publication. Special thanks are due to Subhasis Biswas for garnering the articles for the volume. This is the first Indian reply to the debate on environmental issues in India raised by Western historians. It is expected to be one of the bestsellers on the subject.

Editors

List of Contributors

1.	Ranjan Chakrabarti	Professor of History, Jadavpur University, Kolkata
2.	Aparajita Bhattacharya	Senior Lecturer in History, Thakurpukur Vivekananda College, Kolkata
3.	Subhasis Biswas	Senior Lecturer in History, Jadavpur University, Kolkata
4.	Anindita Majumdar	Senior Lecturer in History, H.L. Pal Memorial College, Konnagar, Hooghly, West Bengal
5.	Sutapa Chatterjee-Sarkar	Reader in History, Brahmananda Keshab Chandra College, Kolkata
6.	Sarmistha Mukherjee	Senior Lecturer in English, Serampur Girls' College, Hooghly, West Bengal
7.	Keka Dutta Roy	Reader in History, Prafulla Chandra College, Kolkata
8.	Kaushik Bandyopadhyay	Lecturer in History, North Bengal University, Raja Rammohunpur, West Bengal
9.	Chittabrata Palit	Professor of History, Jadavpur University, Kolkata

10. Narayan Saha	Reader in History, Moulana Azad College, Kolkata
11. Sukanya Majumdar	Senior Lecturer in History, Navin Bhattacharya Smarak Mahavidyalay, Jalpaiguri, West Bengal
12. Mahua Sarkar	Professor of History, Jadavpur University, Kolkata
13. Rupak Ghoshal	Lecturer in History Nagar College, Jangipur, Murshidabad, West Bengal
14. Chandrakala Dutta	Senior Lecturer in History, Muralidhar Girls' College, Kolkata.

Introduction

Environmental History has gripped the attention of scholars all over the world. In this penultimate round of struggle for coexistence between man and nature, we have arrived at the last stage of survival strategy. Therefore, environmental issues has come to the forefront of all disciplines. History coordinates the views from the past to the future. It provides the hindsight to this emerging area of disconcert to mankind. What were this stages of environmental degradation? What lessons can we draw from the past experience? This volume proves this past for the answer to the future.

In the opening essay on *Understanding the Scope of Environmental History*, **Ranjan Chakrabarti** has rightly focussed on a total approach to the issues and hazards of environment. It embraces climate, ecology, forestry, agriculture, water, irrigation, public health, sanitation, tribal life and literature, peasant resistance, crime and punishment, law and morality – a plethora of issues involving survival in a situation of resource crunch. Environmental history has thus become a nodal subject, argues Chakrabarti.

The next paper, therefore not surprisingly is on the *Chuar Rebellion of 1799 in frontier Bengal* where the author **Aparajita Bhattacharya** takes an ecological approach. The frontier tribal who wants guarded it on behalf of Mughal Emperor and survived here on nature's bounties found with the onset of British rule, official attempt to declare these territories as Company's possession and revenue-bearing. This was resisted by fierce Chuars led by their kings and queens and this led to a veritable struggle for existence-a struggle for space and opportunities on a shrinking frontier.

Subhasis Biswas in the next paper on *Jim Corbett* queries the legendary hunter's so-called love of nature. A notorious killer of alleged man-eaters, he justified his prizes as trophies for the shake of imperilled forest-dwellers. But many a time, it was sheer pastime devastating wildlife and maiming tigers into becoming man-eaters. Corbett also acted as escort to white hunters going for game and procured sherpas for trekking in the mountains.

The theme of colonial desiccation is taken up in the following essay by **Anindita Majumdar** who exposes how *British cupidity for forest timber and revenue led to the decline of flora and fauna* in frontier Southwest Bengal which has not been studied before.

The next string of essays diverts to *representation of nature in literature and art*. **Sutapa Chatterjee-Sarkar** dwells on folk representation of nature in punthis and its urban portrayal in prose. There is a qualitative difference in this transition from inner to outer perspectives from symbiosis to eco-tourism and adventurism. The example cited by her also reveal spiritual to mundane transformation.

Sharmistha Mukherjee also does some kind of deconstruction of elite texts to unravel their concern for environment. She draws illustrations from free Britain and colonial Bengal to contrast between *conservation and destruction*, through the prism of Dickens. Her Bengal part is only a foil to understand Dickensian England.

A thoroughgoing analysis of *pictorial representation of the Bengal famine* of 1943 has been done by **Keka Dutta Roy** in the last essay of this genre. Artists like Somnath Hore, Zainul Abedin or Chittaprasad were eye-witnesses and partial victims of the famine and their paintings vividly portray the calamity cause by a man-made famine. Paintings wonderfully bring out the temporal setting of the famine and famine-victims. It is a silent yet more poignant expression of ecological disaster. Cyclone, flood and scarcity cumulatively caused distortion of human lives as depicted by artists in telling pictures.

Kaushik Bandyopadhyay takes us to the *problem of urban space in 20th century Bengal. Sports and pastime* are part and parcel of a healthy life and there is a notorious dearth of playing grounds in the state and city. There is hardly any space for jogging, not to speak of football which has been used as a symbol by the author to focus our attention on the acute shortage of space. It has not daunted footballers. They make their foray into lanes and by-lanes to play football and energise themselves. There has been no proper town-planning. Every inch of space has been taken up by the unbridled growth of population. The search of space for football popularizes by league and shield football and world cup has led to new kind of environmental awareness.

What is to be done? The next series of essays address this problem. **Chittabrata Palit** in his article reviews the *policy of sanitation of the colonial government* and popular response to it through local self government after the L.S.G. Act of 1920. The popular enthusiasm for a cleaner and healthier space outweighed the government apathy and stringent budget and brought about a sanitary revolution in the rural areas.

Narayan Saha examines the *outcome of earth summits and its incorporation in earth charters*. He highlights this global movement for environmental protection. Sustainable development in an untenable term. Development of any kind means plunder of nature. Over-industrialised nations use this slogan for defending their industrial agenda for greater consumerism. Developing nations should get this advantage to improve their quality of life. The author has raised a very significant debate in this essay.

Sukanya Majumdar is encore with her formulation of a *viable alternative in organic tea-farming* which is compatible with nature. This would stop the process of tea gardens using pesticide for plant protection.

Mahua Sarkar highlights *human rights in weathering environmental crisis*. Attacked from the plank of human rights, enemies of environment will have to retain themselves from destruction of human rights of tribal in the forest in the name of scientific forestry or damming river flow by hydel projects for power for industries at the cost of local landscape and people.

Rupak Ghoshal shows this *conflict between land and people in the forest* areas during the colonial period. Colonial policy not only desiccated forest but also dispossessed its denizens of their habitat.

Chandrakala Dutta moves forward into the *world of globalization and its effects on cosmetic industry*. Suddenly there is an outburst of hectic activities to commercialize herbs and plants for commercial use in the cosmetic industry. It has led to a battle for patents and depletion of our herbal resources.

Together, the essays in this volume open up new vistas of environmental studies which will become a part of the global agenda for the future of mankind. So far this agenda has been at the cost of the third world. This volume presents the Indian vista on this vital question.

1

Understanding the History of Environment

Ranjan Chakrabarti

The study of environmental history has now become important as a natural and inevitable result of a perceived 'environmental crisis' in today's world. This perception has resulted in the development of a broad area called Environmental Studies. However, in view of the important role of the scientists in the emergence of Environmental Studies - and the subsequent contribution of scholars from diverse disciplinary backgrounds to this field - it has remained an open-ended subject. Within the field, 'environmental history' remains universally acknowledged as a critically important area of inquiry, but without well-defined disciplinary canons and methodological guidelines. It is strongly felt that only professional historians with the requisite methodological training will be able to (1) develop and define the agenda and disciplinary canons of this field of inquiry, and (2) historicise the present-day concerns and anxieties in the broad area of Environmental Studies. Unfortunately, professional historians in India and abroad appear to be reluctant to come forward to undertake this task in a concerted and coordinated manner. This is the vacuum that the present essay seeks to fill in.

It is fairly well known that history is essentially a continuous dialogue between the past and the present. Historians give voice to the silences of the archives. The pattern of historical research changes frequently and there is no doubt that it has changed substantially in recent times. It seems that under the forceful impact of post-modernism today we are hearing the voice of alternative histories instead of a simple single track. I am not a post modernist because I do not understand post-modernism very well. But I agree with one of our colleagues (Dr. Sekhar Bandopadhyay) that history has survived the onslaught of post-modernism.[1] The present volume attempts to throw some light on one of the emerging frontiers of historical research. One significant area where the changing approach of historians has yielded smart result is what has come to be called 'history of environment'. The purpose of the present essay is to raise three important questions that the scholars interested in this particular branch of history might wish to ask. These questions are:

(1) Is it a separate sub-discipline under the discipline of history or is it just a recent offshoot of social history/ cultural history / intellectual history/economic history /history from below/ tribal history/history of peasant resistance/history of socio-political crime etc?

(2) What is the present state of scholarship in this field and what is the shape of the historiography of the subject at present?

(3) What could be the strategy or methodology to be pursued by the scholars practising this genre of history?

The present discussion may cater to the needs of those only who have a hazy notion of this particular branch of history. Let us now make a sincere attempt to answer the questions I have already raised.

Defining the Territory

(1) *Is it a separate sub-discipline under the discipline of history or is it just a recent offshoot of social history/cultural history/ intellectual history economic history /history from below/tribal history/ history of peasant resistance/history of socio-political crime etc?*

It has to be admitted that, concern for environment has always been there in human society. South Asia is no exception in this line. In ancient India forests were regarded as abodes of spiritual solace and the concept of preserving forests and wildlife developed around the ashrams of the sages. These forest-based ashrams propagated *aranya sanskriti* or a forest culture and human understanding of the fundamental ecological utility of forest ecosystems and their economic importance, which led to trees and animals being treated with veneration.[2] The ancient texts like the Ramayana give clues to sensibilities. When Rama, the Prince of Ayodhya, is about to set out on his long exile in the forests south of the Gangetic plains, his mother Kaushalya, expresses fears about his safety, 'may the huge elephants not harm you, my dear son, she says, nor the lions, tigers, bears, boars or ferocious horned buffalo'. Rama himself, in a bid to dissuade his wife, Sita, from following him into the woods, paints a similar portrait of the forest as a place of hidden menace. Even the word *vana* or forest was only given to lands where pleasure gave way to hardship. But it is also a place that is beautiful. The twin themes of the forest as a place of dangers to be confronted and of beauty to be enjoyed run like a thread through the epic.[3] The protection of elephants became serious business by the time of the Mauryas. The Arthasastra mentions the rules for protecting the elephant forests. Apart from elephant forests there were other forests where the aim was to secure timber, and tiger and lion skins. The protector of the forest worked to eliminate thieves, tigers and other predators from the woods to make them safe for cattle herders. The same tenor of concern for the wilderness runs through the medieval period. Babur gives much interesting information about wildlife in his memoir. He was a keen observer of wildlife. Interestingly, everywhere the conservationist urge became more pronounced after the industrial revolution. The industrial revolution transformed the rural and urban landscape of Europe. The loss of woodlands and changing landscape created space for ideas of the romantic world of nature. The romantic writings, which were in some ways also a critique of the industrial revolution, celebrated lost nature. It encouraged a back to land movement. William Wordsworth, John Ruskin, William Morris were some of the leading literary figures who contributed to the back to land movement and the setting up of environmental societies in Europe. The rapid disappearance of forest in Europe and America also gave birth to the idea of wilderness, which combined elements of morality, science and aesthetics.[4]

Until the mid-1980s historians have indirectly addressed various environmental or ecological issues while writing economic, social and cultural histories of various types. So, various environmental issues remain scattered in the history of peasant resistance or history from below, agrarian history, tribal history, social and cultural history, history of ideas etc. It is true that such histories concentrated primarily on the arable parts of the landscape with some minor exceptions. This meant that non-arable forest, pastoral, mountain, marsh etc. were, by and large, ignored. Sir Jadunath Sarkar who focused primarily on the political history of the Mughal Empire, writes in detail about the impact of Mughal military expedition to the Indian deep south on the environment. But here as anywhere else references to environmental degradation were made occasionally and rarely. Only in the history of medicine and public health have environmental issues acquired real prominence in historical scholarship before 1980. Some environmental issues do feature in themes like history of crime, conflict over forest laws, movements for folk justice and microscopic studies of popular culture.[5]

We are aware of the recent turns in the pattern of historical research in modern times. The study of environmental history has now become important as a natural and inevitable result of this new shift. The steady expansion of this subject has given it a separate identity as a sub discipline. There has been a tendency to play down the importance of the subject and see it as an integral part of the currently emerging frontier of Environmental Studies. Historians of environment, I will argue, have the responsibility to retain the methodology of their own discipline in their own way. In the process, historians will be better able to contribute to the broader framework of Environmental Studies. I have told you that history as a discipline has survived the onslaught of post-modernism, but it is still necessary to defend the discipline. We shall return to this point later while discussing the third important question relating to this particular branch of history, i.e., methodology.

Brief Historiography

(2) What is the present state of scholarship in this field and what is the shape of the historiography of the subject at present?

Environmental history as a separate subject actually arose in the Euro-American world as an offshoot of the post-war wave of environmentalism. Interestingly the subject was first dragged into the academic arena by natural scientists, who recognised the political and historical significance of their subject, rather than by the historians. The work that set a global agenda for environmental history in 1967 was *Traces on the Rhodian Shore* by Clarence Glacken. Glacken was a geographer and not a historian. Quite a number of scholars, following in Glacken's footsteps, made environmental history intellectually acceptable in the U.S. A major English contribution was *Man and the Natural World* by Keith Thomas (1983). With the publication of Alfred Crosby's *Ecological Imperialism* in 1986, the subject reached another landmark. However, the continents of Asia, Africa hardly featured in any of these works.[6]

Environmental history in Asia and Africa initially derived its strength from the upsurge of the history from below, pioneered by Peter Burke and Thomson and from the increasing interest in material culture so vividly portrayed in the work of Braudel. In fact the *Annale School* (the association of scholars like Marc Bloch, Braudel and Ladourie) has been nurturing the seeds of environmental history since the 1970s though in a different way. They understood that the human experience was the composite result of the interaction of many things, many of which were either autonomous or only partially subject to human volition. They inherited from Durkheim the notion that the individual could only be comprehended within his social context. They thought that the external context could be understood by the same kind of logic as that employed by natural science. This total history was therefore a history that sought a synthesis of all the material, physical and mental forces that had shaped the life of men in the past.[7] Thus, to the scholars of Annale School, the natural environment too, among other things, appeared to be an important consideration in the understanding of the structures of the past.

In South Asia, a basis for environmental history was laid and it began to emerge from the late 1980s. A series of books and articles brought forth this new quest for an environmental history of South Asia. Two of the first of these articles were written by North Americans, Robert K. Winters, a professional forester, the other a radical Indianist political historian-Richard Tucker. Tucker aimed at drawing up a link between nationalist protest and the colonial forest policy in western India.[8] With Tucker's article the whole pace of work changed and in the early 1980s writers from a whole variety of disciplines started to construct a coherent agenda in the environmental history of South and SE Asia. From this time onwards environmental history and forest history of India, in particular, became intensely politicised. The process of politicisation had begun with the rise of the Chipko Movement in northern India. In the 1980s and 1990s two important questions kept the environmental historians on their toes: (1) What was the real history of protest against state forestry in India and in what ways was it connected to the broad history of nationalist protest? (2) What was the ideological history of the state agency that was threatening the ecology of India? The debate that took off regarding a fresh forest act in 1980 freed the historians from their earlier indifference to the subject. Quite a number of scholars stationed in India, the Duke University (John Richards, Haynes) and Oxford approached the subject from different directions. While the Duke project concentrated more on agrarian changes and land use in the tropics and its impact on environment, researchers in India concentrated on the history of resistance to colonial forest policy and the ideological content of that policy. [9]

Ramchandra Guha in his articles and subsequently in his books [10] asserted that in the pre-British period there was little or no interference with the customary use of forest and forest produce.

Thus, Guha views colonial forest policy and conservation as primarily driven by materialistic considerations that of serving the strategic and revenue interest of the British Empire. In opposition to the argument propounded by Gadgil and Guha that imperial needs for timber and shipbuilding propelled scientific forestry with its associated bureaucracy. Richard Grove argues that colonial conservationism was based on humanist concerns motivated by growing deforestation and drought. (Richard Grove argues that it was desiccationism that promoted the idea of forest conservancy in the colonies. Desiccationism draws on the connection between deforestation and drought, shrinking water resources, soil erosion and productivity etc.).[11] The officials of the European trading companies were able to take note of them. These people systematically developed the desiccationist discourses and sought state intervention in the protection of forests. In the process, Grove plays down the importance of imperialist or capitalist greed behind the forest policy and focuses on other considerations, which were more humane. Mahesh Rangarajan[12] does not see simple polarities between the two sets of ideas and suggests that a convergence of ideas was indeed the case. He argues that the desiccationist fear had only a limited impact and was only one of the influences that shaped the course of the early 19th century Indian forestry. Ajay Skaria[13] views forest conservancy that emerged out of the desiccationist discourses also as a part of the broader 'civilising mission' of imperialism. Skaria disagrees with Grove and says that the agenda of forest conservancy was not 'innocent of colonial domination'. In a recent article DD Dangwal[14] followed up the view of Skaria and shows how desiccationism was frequently used by the state to extend control over the central Himalayan forests (Uttaranchal).

I see the problem as essentially an integral part of a broader strategy of power which was geared primarily to ensure the domination of the Indian colony by its white rulers. To the British rulers, the colonisation of India seemed to be incomplete without the pacification of the jungle. To them the Indian jungle alone had the wilderness to match the valour of the masculine occident.[15]

The Forest Acts, in a single stroke, made government's claim over the forest legitimate, and hunting, food gathering or cutting trees became illegitimate. The main group of offences was that of hunting, wounding or stealing of animals, and poaching or fishing. In this manner was created a whole new legal category of forest crimes. There was a progressive criminalisation of varied forms of human activity within the Indian jungle which were previously not under the purview of the state. The legislators, throughout the colonial period were constantly extending the boundaries of forest crimes, though the popular perception of what constituted 'forest crime' still remained very fluid. The government's claim over the forest was displayed as just and legitimate. The new forest policy was geared to generate a new sensibility as to the use of forests. There is no disagreement on the point that the forest was destroyed due to the policy of ruthless commercial exploitation adopted by the colonial government. The British first destroyed the forest and then became the self-styled protectors of the forest. I have argued elsewhere that the English were the real poachers but they used the game law to brand the indigenous forest people, who earned their livelihood from the forest, as 'poachers'. The indigenous people, being deprived of their age old forest rights, often refused to recognize the validity of government's claims and they continued to cultivate at will, cut trees and burn the forest floors as they had been doing since times immemorial. Thus, having destroyed the animals the European hunters later emerged as self-styled conservationists and went flat out to romanticize the tropical rain forest and its animals.[16]

Grove rejects the Guha-thesis as 'a golden age' approach to South Asian environmental history and questions the assumptions about the existence of pre-colonial common property and communal customary forest use. The recent research of Rangarajan, Skaria, Damodaran and others certainly took some of its cues from the early works of Tucker and the subalternists. But it has been also influenced by the globalist approach of Alfred Crosby[17] and the revisionism of Christopher Bayly.[18] Bayly has encouraged some of the environmental historians to treat colonial rule not as a watershed but as a period in which continuities with the pre-colonial period, were to be regarded as important. Grove also sees the bias in South Asian environmental history caused by an overemphasis on the post-1857 period. Both Mahesh Rangarajan and Grove rightly pointed to the significance of the forest policies pursued by the successor states to the Mughals. Grove in particular draws our attention to the need of a comprehensive history of drought, famine and climatic changes. In considering the impact of climatic change on the history of this region we have advanced very little so far. It is perhaps in this area of research that we can expect to see most movement in the environmental history of South Asia in the coming years. This inclination has already surfaced in some of the essays in the volume edited by Grove and others.[19]

Methodology

(3) What could be the strategy or methodology to be pursued by the scholars practising this genre of history?

Knowledge is considered as knowledge only when it is methodologically obtained. History is a piece of knowledge as it is obtained through a definite methodology. The practitioners of the discipline are expected to practise the discipline according to certain methods. Like any other histories, here too, it is necessary for the historian to concentrate on the collection of primary and secondary sources and the selection and interpretation of such sources. As to choice of subjects historians are usually attracted by silences or slippages in the writing of history. Environmental history is a new area and here such slippages and silences are understandably too many. They now await their historians. I will argue that environmental history does not call for any separate methodology; the basic tenets of the discipline remain very much valid in this sub-discipline of the history of environment. It might however require specific strategies, tactics and some preliminary knowledge of environmental sciences on the part of the historian to negotiate particular issues depending on the subject or the nature of his or her research.

I have mentioned earlier that there has been a tendency to play down the importance of the subject and see it as an integral part of the currently emerging frontier of Environmental Studies. There are certain misconceptions as to the respective territories of history of environment and environmental studies. It is important to clear these misconceptions to foster historical researches in this field. There is a general misconception that natural scientists are better equipped than historians to contribute to this particular branch of knowledge. It has to be admitted that the roots of this misconception can be attributed to the initial indifference of historians to the subject. Before 1980 the historians had considered environmental subjects to be of dubious value. The historians initially could not contribute much to this new frontier of environmental studies. Interestingly enough, environmental history was first forced into the academic arena by the natural scientists who recognised the political and historical significance of their subject. To make matters worse, the agenda of environmental history was actually drawn up by scholars from various disciplines and not by the historians. The methodological uncertainty of history of environment has stemmed from this initial inertia of historians. The problem has, in course of time, triggered off another misconception, i.e., it is widely held that environmental history has to be necessarily inter-disciplinary in nature. Even historians engaged in environmental history are not completely free from this misconception. It is true that historians engaged in environmental history should have rudimentary knowledge of such basic concepts like ecosystem, atmosphere, hydrosphere, lithosphere, biosphere, epidemic diseases, medical science, forestry, climate, soil, vegetation, fauna etc., but such borrowing of knowledge from other disciplines does not necessarily make environmental history an interdisciplinary field. When the methodologies of two or more disciplines combine to produce a fresh methodology, only then we can call it an interdisciplinary study. The notion that experts from the natural sciences are better placed to pursue environmental history; history of medicine or history of science has little substance. Such notions actually are the result of absolute lack of historical sense from which many scientists unfortunately suffer. I have heard an eminent scientist saying in a public seminar, 'you have to be a scientist to write history of science' (according to this logic one has to be a peasant to write peasant history or one has to be a criminal to pursue history of crime). Little do they realise that history too has its methodology and you need some training in that discipline to become a historian. This is why in most cases what they produce at the end of the road is nothing more than mere chronicles or mere stories of scientific inventions. Historians of environment, I will therefore argue, have the responsibility to retain the methodology of their own discipline in their own way. In the process, historians will be better able to contribute to the broader framework of Environmental Studies.

The appellations of all the various branches of history are labels of convenience rather than names of essences. The phrase environmental history is no exception. Environment is a broad term, which encompasses all that surrounds us, both the natural world in which we live as well as the technology of production and things produced by us. In this sense all histories can be viewed as environmental history. However in actual fact we make a distinction between environmental history and other histories. The historiography of the history of environment shows that in environmental history there is an emphasis on various ecological factors and their impact on the history of a particular region. An external force, substance or condition that surrounds and affects the life of an organism in any way, becomes a factor of its environment and is called an environmental or ecological issue. Historians might be of some help in mapping out the social, economic and cultural impact of the changes in the ecosystem. An ecosystem can be defined as the grouping of various kinds of plants, animals and microorganisms interacting with each other and with their environment. Thus an ecosystem consists of living organisms and the physical environment in which they live. Grassland, a forest, a pond or a lake may be considered an ecosystem. A historical study of an ecosystem is ecological history or environmental history. It is important for the environmental historian to remember that unlike other branches of history it may not remain confined to a strictly guarded chronological framework; shorter periods may not be ideal for ecological histories, on the contrary, the emphasis here is on long *duree*. I have already said that in a sense all histories can be viewed as environmental history.

Environment is a broad term, which encompasses all that surrounds us. Environmental history is pregnant with immense possibilities. There is a wonderful opportunity to undertake various social, economic, cultural and intellectual histories under the umbrella of environmental history and explore such themes like race, ethnicity, class, community, gender, power, knowledge etc. One could see, for example, how the jungle or the Indian forest became an important site for the interplay of various forces like racism, colonialism, nationalism and struggle for equality during British colonialism in India. It is understandable that the forest became one of the important social sites for the exercise of colonial power and for the domination and inferiorisation of the 'Indian other'. I have argued elsewhere that it is possible to comprehend the implication of the exercise of power in various social and cultural sites or spaces when social construction of space is viewed historically.[20] The historical transformation of space as container of power can only be identified when we study discourses in their dialectical interaction with the dynamic of human agency or producers or architects of such discourses. I have shown in one of my recent articles how in the course of the 19th century the forest turned into an important venue where the Euro-American selves and the Indian Others started interacting.[21]

The choice of the subject of research is indeed the unique autonomy of the historian.[22] But here for the sake of discussion I can suggest certain gateways for environmental histories. I do not intend to say these gateways are ideal or that these are the only methods, which have to be necessarily followed. This is only a tentative set of options, which may be of some help to open up this particular frontier. The themes mentioned here are all interlinked and overlapping:

(1) Social, economic, cultural and intellectual histories under the umbrella of environmental history and study of themes like race, ethnicity, class, community, gender, power, knowledge etc. Richard Grove documents the profound dependence of Western ideas about the natural world upon the knowledge of people living in the colonial periphery,

showing especially how 'the seeds of modern conservation developed as an integral part of the European encounter with the tropics and with local classifications and interpretation of the natural world and its symbolisms'.[23]

(2) History of Environment comprises forest, deforestation, soil erosion, resistance, politics of environment, subsistence, the animal and the insect world in tropical forests, hunting or shikar, poaching, forest crime, smuggling etc. Recent approach to hunting provides an important theme in history. The killing of animals is associated with ideological overtones and both text and pictorial art have tended to emphasize the mystic, courtly and martial rather than the purely narrative side of the chase. The European hunters of the nineteenth and twentieth centuries were aware of this rich tradition and turned hunting into a symbolic activity within the study of natural history, a central area of scientific debate in the period. Hunting had its assigned place in the social and economic system. It was subject to complex legislation and was much influenced by technical developments in firearms. If we look at development of human society we find three different typologies in hunting: (1) subsistence hunting, (2) defence hunting and (3) hunting as sport or pleasure[24] Subsistence hunting was an important economic activity among primitive men who lived primarily on a food gathering-hunting economy. Even among those communities who are peasantised and all set for settled agriculture, hunting offers a subsidiary economic activity. Many primitive or tribal communities in India, who are peasantised, still rest on hunting to a considerable extent. Again, hunting for meat interestingly coexists with relatively advanced stages of production and to a limited extent, the practice survives even today. Defence hunting means killing or trapping of animals (deer, wild boar, monkey, elephant, bison, tiger etc.) for the protection of crops and human lives. Defence hunting, understandably, occupied a greater part of human activity when larger areas were under forests and technology, particularly weaponry were at a primitive stage.[25] In some

areas of post-colonial India however, protection of crops or human lives still remain as one of the major problems for the local people and forest officials in India and elsewhere in South Asia. Hunting as pleasure or sport acquired importance with the advent of relatively advanced stages of civilization[26] and continues in some form or other to the present day, despite the fact that legislators in recent times had been continuously expanding the frontier of law to ensure conservation and scientific management of forests all over the world. Study of the animal world too can give important dues to sensibilities. I have tried to unveil the amazing fact how the colonial authorities and the Bengal tiger seemed to be locked in a conflict for command of the Sundarbans. Thus the big cat turned into a site for the demonstration of colonial power.

(3) Climate, impact of climatic changes on history, demography, natural calamities, earthquake, cyclonic storms, flood, rainfall, volcanic eruptions etc.

(4) Air and water pollution, history of sound and smell (Alain Corbin, *The Foul and the Fragrant,* 1986).

(5) History of public health, epidemics, medicine.

Concluding Remarks

There is no disagreement on the point that colonial forest policy was not geared to bring welfare to the colonized people. The 'scientific forestry' never appeared to be fruitful in the colonial context. The legacy of failure in the domain of forest policy continues unabated in the post-colonial period. The ideology of conservation itself today faces a crisis. Smugglers and poachers, supported by political and business interests and sheltered by local communities, raid the protected forests for valuable exports, killing elephants for their tusks and tigers for their skins. The scientific forestry has alienated the indigenous population settled near the forest zones. They are hostile to the idea of conservation. This is precisely why the smugglers and the poachers are able to operate at ease. They can, if necessary, slip into the fold of popular concealment and resentment of decades enable them to evade the law. The official forest policy has excluded local people from protected areas, it has deprived them of the right to use the forest and it has preserved the forest only for the animals. To ensure the success of the project, it is necessary to integrate the local people in the project of conservation. Local knowledge and resources can be used only through a participatory policy involving the people. The inability of the Forest Department to improve the condition of forests has forced it to opt for participatory management - joint forest management or JFM. Under JFM the forest department involves village communities in forest management. Village forest committees have been formed under JFM. This is showing some positive results. But the domination of the government officials stays. It is necessary to democratise the JFM, so as to involve the people in the decision making process. To achieve success, we have to change our approach. The forest should not be looked upon as merely a source of various products or as an object of protection. Nature lovers continue to visit to the National Parks, hoping to see tigers in Ranthambor or rare birds in Bharatpur. Forest officials congratulate themselves on the rapid population increase of many threatened species. It is necessary to humanize the forests and adopt a more humane approach to the people and their way of life. The forest department has to remember that in the ultimate analysis the forests should serve the needs of the people.

Nature is one of those spaces where we observe the most intense form of class struggle and power politics. Those who are more privileged control more than 70% of the natural resources across the world. The same is true about the developed nations of the world as far as the use of the natural world is concerned. Thus it has to be appreciated that history of environment would serve as one of the important gateways to knowledge in general and environmental studies in particular. It will lead the historians to areas hitherto unexplored, raise questions hitherto unasked, penetrate into the mysterious pathways of the mental world of the common people and disclose how the attitudes to environment change in keeping with the changing structure of culture and ideology. History of environment, therefore, does matter. It is in this area of environmental history that we may expect to see most intense activity in the near future. I have no doubt that environmental history is packed with immense possibilities. A day will come when all histories will be looked upon as environmental history. That day is not very far off. Environmental history will continue to thrive because the seeds of a social history is firmly embedded in it. This history will be free from the riddles of the so called 'post-modernist' exercises of recent times and will be certainly richer and more readable.

Notes and References

1. Sekhar Bandopadhyay (ed.), *Rethinking History,* Delhi, 2001, pp. 12-16.
2. A.S. Rawat, *A History of Forestry in India,* Delhi, 1991, p. 130.
3. R.P. Goldman (ed.), *The Ramayana of Valmiki : An Epic of Ancient India,* vol. II, The Ayodhyakanda, Princeton, 1986, pp. 131-136.
4. Madhav Gadgil and Ramchandra Guha, *This Fissured Land : An Ecological History of India,* Delhi, 1992, passim; also Gadgil and Guha, State Forestry and Social Conflict in British India in David Hardiman (ed.), *Peasant Resistance in India* 1858-1914, Delhi, 1993, pp. 259-295.
5. Cf. Hobsbawm, *Primitive Rebels,* Manchester, 1974, *Bandits,* Harmondsworth, 1985;
   E.P. Thomson, *Whigs and Hunters,* Harmondsworth, 1975, Albion's *Fatal Tree: Crime and Society in 18th century England,* 1975;
   J.C. Scott, *The Moral Economy of the Peasant: Rebellion and Subsistence in Southeast Asia,* Yale, 1976 etc.
6. Richard Grove et al, *Nature and the Orient: The Environmental History of South and South East Asia,* OUP, New Delhi.
7. Ranjan Chakrabarti, Foucault and the New Social History, *Journal of History (Jadavpur University), Vol. XI,* 1990-91.
   Jacques Le Goff and P. Nora (eds), *Constructing the Past: Essays in Historical Methodology,* Cambridge, 1985.
8. Richard Tucker, *Forest Management and Imperial Politics, Indian Economic and Social History Review,* 1979.

9. Richard Grove (eds), *Nature and the Orient,* op.cit., p. 16.
10. Ramchandra Guha, op.cit.
11. Richard Grove, op.cit., see also *Green Imperialism: Colonial Expansion, Tropical Edens and the Origins of Environmentalism,* 1995; *Ecology, Climate and Empire,* 1998.
12. Mahesh Rangarajan, *Fencing the Forest : Conservation and Ecological Change in India's Central Provinces,* Delhi, 1996.
13. Ajay Skaria, *Hybrid Histories: Forests, Frontiers and Wilderness in Western India,* Delhi, 1999.
14. D.D. Dhangwal, *Scientific Forestry and Forest Management in Colonial and Postcolonial India, Contemporary India, Vol. I,* 2001.
15. Ranjan Chakrabarti, *The Jungle, the Imperial Hunt and British Imperialism 1800-1947* in C. Palit and A. Bhattacharyya (eds), *Science, Technology, Medicine and Environment,* Calcutta, 1998; Colonising the Forest 1800-1900, Sukumar Bhattacharya (ed.), *Mountains and Forests in Indian History,* Kolkata, 2005, Tiger and the Raj: Ordering the Maneater of the Sundarbans : 800-1947, Ranjan Chakrabarti (ed.), *Space and Power in History,* Kolkata, 2001.
16. Ibid.
17. Alfred W. Crosby, *Ecological Imperialism : The Biological Expansion of Europe 900-*1900, Cambridge, 2004 (new edition).
18. Christopher and Susan Bayly, Eighteenth-century State Forms and the Economy, *Arrested Development in India,* Delhi, 1988.
19. Richard Grove (ed.), *Nature and the Orient,* op.cit.
20. Ranjan Chakrabarti (ed.), *Space and Power in History*, op.cit.
21. Ranjan Chakrbarti, op.cit.
22. E.H. Carr, What is History? New York, 1961, pp. 51-55.
23. Richard Grove, *Green* Imperialism, op.cit.
24. J.M. Mackenzie, *The Empire of Nature,* Manchester, 1988, passim.
25. J.K. Anderson, *Hunting in the Ancient World,* Berkeley, 1981, pp.1-16.
26. Anderson, op.cit.

2

The Chuar Rebellion of 1799 : An Ecological Approach

Aparajita Bhattacharya

The forest tracts of South-West Bengal has remained a disturbed area since the advent of the British rule in that area. The tribals and aborigines of this area, popularly known as the Jungle Mahals, offered resistance to the establishment of the British rule throughout the late 18th and 19th centuries. These resistance movements are generally considered as examples of primitive resistance. The historiographical explanations of these movements have so far emphasized the political and socio-economic aspects of these movements. The purpose of this essay is to find out an ecological explanation of these struggles. To begin with, I have tried to study the late 18th century developments in the area for the present essay and more particularly the Chuar Uprising of 1799. My purpose is to relate the ecological degeneration of the area with the political developments. Hence I will not describe the event in the detail but will try to place it in the broader perspective of ecological change.

The very name 'Jungle Mahals' suggests that it was a place beyond settlement. Due to absence of enough cultivable land,

Jungle Mahals was always sparsely populated. Majority of the inhabitants were aboriginal tribes. The tribes met herewith were the Bhars, Bhumijs, Gonds, Santals, Kharias, Kols, Nats, puraons, Sabars and Dhangars or Uraon.[1] Of these tribes, the Bhumjs and Santals formed the bulk of the population. The British Lieutenants found that the inhabitants of this area were mostly *Paiks* who had a hierarchy of *Sardars* (headmen), *Khandaits* (swordsmen) and *Chuars*. These *Chuars* were mostly Bhumij people and were probably the autochthones or original inhabitants of the Jungle Mahals.

It is necessary to mention a few aspects of Bhumij socio-cultural and economic life in order to understand the role of forestry in their life. The Bhumij people mainly followed a hunter-gatherer mode of economic life and occasionally practised shifting cultivation.[2] They were the source of the militia of Jungle zamindars and held lands in service tenures described as paikan, ghatwali, and chakeran tenures. The superior knowledge of the jungle and hill tracts made them an effective guerilla force. They were brave, industrious and much attached to their proprietors. Occasional trade of sal resin, mahua flowers, lac, tasar cocoons, wax, herbal plants, roots, honey and other forest products other than timber formed a part of the economic life of these Bhumij people.[3]

The Zamindars of this area were described by the British officials as rude and illiterate. Sometimes they were the local people while in some cases they came from outside and imposed themselves over the existing forest tribes.[4] They organized cultivation by mobilizing tribals and migrant peasants and participated in the trade of jungle products.

The socio-cultural life of these tribal people also very much depended upon the forestry around them. The rituals of marriage were performed before the branches of Mahua and Sidha trees. Similarly a divorce was indicated by tearing apart a wet Sal leaf. The mass of the people worshipped the Sun under the name of *Sin-Bonga* and *dharam* as the giver of harvests to men. They also worshipped a host of other gods like, *Karakata*, *Baghut*, *Buru*,

Gram-deota etc. some of these were agricultural deities, while *Baghut* protected them from tiger and *Buru* was mountain deity. [5] The most popular festival of the Bhumij people was the *Karam* festival where a branch of Karam trees was planted in the village dancing ground. At the foot of this branch a vessel, partly filled with earth and various seed grains were kept. By the last day of the month, the seeds germinated and the girls danced whole night. All these facts show that the Bhumij tribe was very much connected to the natural environment around them.

In the pre-colonial era the Jungle Mahals was formally under the Mughal control. [6] But due to the density of the forest and inaccessibility of the area little attempts were made to extract revenue or exert a direct control. As a result the tribal people of this area maintained their unique socio-economic practices and identity for hundreds of years without remarkable change. The demands of the agrarian society for expansion of arable lands resulted in clearance of the forest areas to some extent. But the core areas of the forest remained unaltered, only the boundaries, shifted.

This subsistence oriented isolationist life of the tribals of the Jungle Mahals faced a threat of vigorous change after 1760. By a treaty of 27th September 1760, Mir Qasim Ali in return for his appointment of Nawab Nazim, made a grant to the English East India Company of the three districts of Chittagong, Burdwan and Midnapore. From 1767 onwards the Midnapore Residents sent military expeditions to Jungle Mahals, which was then a part of the district, in an attempt to extract revenue and exert, effective political control over the area.

The changes brought about by the colonial intervention must be viewed in the context of the social changes within Britain. With the beginning of agricultural revolution in England, the cutting of trees and the cultivation of wasteland were taken to be signs of progress. Through the 17th and 18th centuries forest dwellers in England were locked in struggles with the crown official and larger landlords over control of the woodlands. From around 1750 English landowners planted trees on privately owned and enclosed lands.[7] The woods became a managed and controlled landscape rather than an untamed forest.

In India the early British rulers hoped to consolidate their control by extending cultivation. Basic principles of colonial state-making also played a role here. State-making refers to the ideology and organizational power of the Central Govt. to penetrate rural society, exact compliance and invoke commitment.[8] Increase in colonial information about forest areas, vermin eradication, demilitarization of forest chiefs, sedentarisation of forest tribes etc. were forms of state making. In short, forests were a land to be conquered and tamed. Not only the forest line now would often be in retreat, but the new political context led a tilt against groups on the fringes of settled agriculture.

Military campaigns and high revenue assessments were used to carve out of the impenetrable and inscrutable jungle first encountered. The clearing of wastelands for cultivation was given priority. English collectors were to ascertain the collections from ryots and the quantity of cultivated and wasteland in every pargana. But these measures did not yield expected dividend because there were no people to clear the wastelands and extend cultivation. People of the lowlands, did not rise to inducement to settle in the Jungle Mahals.[9]

Gaining a closer acquaintance with the forests through these experiences, Company officials realized much about at ternate econonomic values that the forest might hold. Lieutenant Fergusson, in charge of the expedition to the Jungle Mahals wrote to the Resident of Midnapore in February, 1767, "I understand they have abundance of wax, oil dammar, buffaloes, besides the capital article of timber..."[10] By the late 1780s and 1790s the travellers' journals did occasionally mention encountering *teak*, *sal* and *sissoo* forests, all Indian timbers by then widely recognized as commercially valuable. The major initiative, however, flowed from the strategic and commercial imperatives of a transcontinental empire. South Asia acquired a new significance in the context of

Anglo-French rivalry and the need to tap new sources of wood for shipping. Naval rivalry accentuated the problem of the shortage of timber within Britain.[11] The issue of obtaining adequate timber for ships led to the first steps for the control of the use of forests.

All these show that whether for expansion of arable or to fulfill the commercial demands of the expanding British Empire forest were to be cut and terrain tamed. The British Occupation of the Jungle Mahals, however, never went unchallenged. The British troops were met with all round non-cooperation. The forest chieftains and tribal communities resisted ambushing British forces and harassing them whenever possible. In 1799, a widespread violent rebellion broke out in this region, which the British authorities named as Chuar Rebellion. In spite of much initial resistance the British, however, through their superior force gradually succeeded in extending their control in the area. Colonial law and political control were grafted on an indigenous tribal society.

Throughout the 19th century the Colonial rulers exploited the Jungle lands by systematic deforestation. The negative consequences of the degradation of forests had to be felt before any preventive action was taken. It is true that every period in Indian History had its own forest line besides its political and military boundaries. But customary restraints on the use of trees had earlier ensured renewal. Now to cater the revenue and strategic needs of trans-continental empire, forestry was destroyed to a scale hitherto unknown in the sub-continent. In the course of years in a country where the soil is shallow and unbroken rock very near the surface, the soil deprived of the binding force of the tree roots, tends to get washed off the slopes into the valleys by the torrential rains. Hence streches of absolutely barren land appeared and siltation of rivers took place.

If we consider the Chuar Rebellion as a clash between the private and the civilized, a clash of culture, of ways of life, then the character of the struggle appears to be a socio-economic and cultural struggle. If we consider the motive of the local elitist leaders behind the launching of the movement, it takes up a political colour.

With due consideration to these views I wish to add that this struggle can also be explained from an ecological point of view. We have seen that forestry supplied the day-to-day needs of the forest communities. Their belief systems were strongly ground in the worship of nature. Their religious festivals were tied to both the agricultural cycle and flowering and fruiting of the forest trees. Their festival songs depict a close link between the health of the forest, fertility and prosperity. The aborigines belonged to hunter-gatherer form of society and sometimes practised shifting cultivation. Thus, their subsistence was supplied by local forestry. Protection of nature or forestry, therefore, meant protection of deities, of deep-rooted religious beliefs and of means of subsistence to these primitive people. In this way their struggle obviously had an environmental or ecological side, as protection of nature was one important sentiment.

It must not be assumed that these primitive people were environment conscious in a way we today are. But every aspect of their life was connected with nature. And to them a loss of control and direct contact with nature meant loss of everything. From this feeling of loss or helplessness on the onslaught of colonialism they took up arms to protect their mother nature. It was a frantic effort on their part, but an effort indeed. It is true that their struggle cannot be characterized as a purely ecological one. However, if we take up the aborigines as a part of the ecological cycle of the Jungle Mahals area, the ecological explanation becomes more direct. These people cut trees and also protected them and planted new ones. They killed animals and themselves also got killed by them. They killed smaller animals and birds for food and their killing of ferocious animals kept the latter's number within a manageable limit. Therefore, the local human inhabitants played a very important role in maintaining the ecological balance of the area. Only thing is that they were not overtly conscious about this fact.

Here we come to the next part of our argument, i.e., the role of the outer elements. As we have seen the people of the Jungle Mahals very rarely came in close contact with the outside world. They were not ready to take the outsiders in their confidence.

Therefore, the ideas and ideologies of outsiders could not mobilize them till this time.

This contact with the outer world was effectively established only in the 20th century. The result was an effective mobilization of tribals demands by the outsiders. As a consequence, the ecological and environmental issues came in the forefront and the struggles and conflicts with the state now can be explained from the ecological point of view. Had this contact been established earlier the Chuar Rebellion might also have a direct ecological colour. I like to conclude by saying that as students of History we all know that it is time that brings out the ultimate change. In this case also it is a time period of more than 200 years that has moulded the issues, ideas and our views to give a new interpretation of a much-discussed event of history.

Notes and References

1. Hunter, W.W., *A Statistical Account of Bengal*, Vol – III, Part –I (Midnapore), (London 1876, Reprint 1997), p.37.
2. K.Sivaramakrishnan, *Modern Forests : State Making and Environmental Change in Colonial Eastern India*, (Delhi, 1999), p.48.
3. Ibid.
4. Hiteshranjan Sanyal, *Continuities of Social Mobility in Traditional and Modern Societies in India: Two case studies of caste Mobility in Bengal*, Journal of Asian Studies, Vol-30 (2), pp 321-26.
5. H.H. Risley. *The Tribes and Castes of Bengal*, Vol. – I (Calcutta, 1891) p.127.
6. L.S.S.O'Malley, *Bengal District Gazetteer : Midnapore*, (Calcutta, 1910, Reprint 1995), p. 23.
7. Mahesh Rangarajan, *Imperial Agendas and India's Forests: The early History of Indian Forestry, 1800-1878*, Indian Economic and Social History, Review, Vol-31, No.II, April-June 1994, pp. 147-167.
8. K.Sivaramakrishnan, *British imperium and forested Zones of anomaly in Bengal, 1767-1833* IESHR, Vol-33, No.II, April-June, 1996, pp. 244-246.
9. Ibid.

10. W.K. Firminger (ed.). *Bengal District Records: Midnapore*, Vol-I, Letter no. 124, (Calcutta, 1926). pp.95-96.
11. Ramachandra Guha & Madhav Gadgil, *This Fissured Land : An Ecological History of India*, (Delhi, 1992), p.119.

3

Jim Corbett and His Love for Nature : A Critical Review from the Perspective of the History of Indian Environment

Subhasis Biswas

From a self-conceived cultural superiority and political domination, the people of the West initiated adventure to the mysterious world of the forests of the orient with a conscious knowledge fever of their own. The journey to the world of 'fixed ethnic stereotypes – 'the tribes' widened the knowledge of the British about the society and economy of the 'conquered people', particularly in the forest areas. In this knowledge gathering stage the people from the occident slowly created the idea of an 'oriental world', treated this world as 'other world' and found an unknown species 'the tribes' as a taxonomic device of this 'other world'. Here other world means a world in the oriental forest away from the civilized society with a different culture and ideology. It was the white man's burden to civilize the people of this 'other world'. But in the mind of many Europeans, there was a fusion between these two worlds - civilized world of the West and barbaric world of the oriental forests. Some Europeans, who were born in India and closely associated with Indian forests, were influenced by both the European values and also some values of the Indian society. Jim Edward Corbett, who was born in Nainital in 1875 and stayed almost seventy years in India had a deep love for this country and its people. But the self-contradiction as manifested in his treatment of the 'people of the forest' and especially the environmental issues of the forests reveals a different story. The present paper highlights the inner duality of an European's mind in the colonial context of the late nineteenth and early twentieth century India.

Edward James Corbett was born in Nainital on 25 July, 1875. He was the twelfth child of his mother, Mary Jane Corbett and eighth of his father Christopher William Corbett.[1] The family of Jim Corbett was very large indeed even by the standard of the day. His father was the post-master of Nainital. Corbett's father was the man who was directly involved in many of the deforestation activities sponsored by the Nainital municipal body. Before 1860s there were dense forest areas around Nainital. But after the settlement of the Europeans a large area was cleared by them to build new houses. Christopher William Corbett was one of the Europeans engaged in these activities. He purchased many plots of land on the hill slopes of the town and he built many cottages in these plots. He used to sell these plots judiciously from time to time, reinvesting in other plots as these became available and accessible by brittle tracks and roads.[2] This process of urbanization helped the destruction of ecological balance in Nainital.[3] Corbett's father was directly involved in these types of activities.[4] In the first forest Act of 1865 some restrictions were imposed to check this rapid deforestation in the Himalayan areas and in the second forest Act of 1878 these restrictions became more rigid. But according to the British colonial mentality no law was seriously applied against the Europeans.[5] This phenomenon ultimately created an ecological crisis which was proved by increasing number of landslides.[6] In 1880s, a devastating landslide took place in Nainital.[7] It did not only severe damages but also changed the pattern of urbanization in Nainital. The calamity was best described by a local government officer in the Kumaon Gazetteer :

"The rain commenced to fall steadily and without cessation from Thursday the 16th September, 1880 until Sunday evening, the l9th. The rain was accompanied by violent gusts of wind from the east; the roads were injured, the water courses choked, and there was a general saturation of the soil in all places where the loose debris of rotten shade, of which the northern ridge is composed, allowed the water to penetrate. There was much clearing of new sites during the previous years and the builders did not always provide for the derangement of natural drainage channel's."[8]

The landslide was terrifying and catastrophic. 151 people including 43 Europeans died.[9] But the reason for which the landslide happened was more important. The calamity sounded a distinct warning of ecological imbalance. The Nainital Gazetteer, clearly mentioned that the clearing of a major forest area was the reason for this large scale deforestation. The European settlement destroyed the natural drainage system in Nainital, which was also one of the main reasons of landslide.[10] Sir Henry Ramsay, the Commissioner of Nainital at this time, quickly arranged a totally new drainage scheme and no similar devastation occurred since.[11] But the ecological balance was lost for ever. Christopher William Corbett was one of the leading Europeans who cleared the forest areas to open more lands for settlement. His better known son inherited this practice and he supplied timber to the railway companies in later years.

For the first few years of his life, Jim lived in the style of any European child in India. It was a privileged childhood for any European, no matter what was their place in the hierarchy of the expatriate society. Servants were plentiful, incredibly loyal and extremely cheap.[12] Corbett's mother, Mary Jane Corbett was an active woman and engaged in various business activities. A discussion on Corbett's childhood expresses how Corbett became an ideal European from his childhood, which helped to shape his ideology in later years. He was in touch with Indian society from his childhood, but ideology of a white man always kept him away from the Indian values.

Jim was always in care of the Indian servants from his childhood. This led to the servants 'educating' the children in local tongues, etiquette and for want of a better term, 'native knowledge', which covered every topic of Indian life, from religion to superstitions. From the servants Jim learnt much about Indian religion. He picked up the local language and could easily speak the Kumaoni dialect: With equal ease he also picked up the local superstitions of the Kumaonis.[13]

In spite of such early Indian influence in him, Corbett retained his European identity because he learnt his mother tongue from his mother and an elder sister and went to a school (Oak Opening) founded by a retired officer of the Indian Army where he learnt about the cultural and military superiority of the white people.[14] His training as a cadet also helped him retain his European identity. Corbett wrote that in his childhood days his dream was to become a perfect British soldier. In his later years, Corbett joined the British Army during the First World War. Thus he received his first training in colonial hegemony since his school days.[15]

Although Corbett had a very strong European identity from his childhood days, his interaction with the common people of India and his attachment with the forests of Kumaon cannot be neglected. Thus he had a particularly warm relation with Kunwar Singh, the headman of Chandni Chaulk village from his childhood days. He learnt much about nature from Kunwar Singh.[16] Hunting was not banned in this forest area in the 1870s and 1880s.[17] But contrarily there were many forests reserved exclusively for hunting by the Maharaja and the Europeans. Only Kings and Europeans were allowed to display their shooting prowess in this area.[18] In Kumaon, the dense forest near Kaladhungi was one of these forest reserves and Henry Ramsay, the Commissioner of Kumaon was in charge of this forest reserve. Corbett later mentioned this forest area as 'Governmental forest'.[19] The original dwellers of this forest land had no right of hunting there. Hence, Kunwar Singh, in Corbett's view, was a poacher, while Tom, his elder brother was 'a great hunter'.[20] This sharp contrast was very clear to Jim Corbett from his childhood days. At this time, maharajas, viceroys, senior army officials and other influential Europeans attended massive shoots, sometimes killing even as many as six tigers in a day.[21] The poor Indians helped the hunters in this 'organised hunting', by beating drums, chasing the animals and in many other different ways. Jim mentioned this Kumaoni forest area as 'a happy hunting ground'. [22] At the age of twelve, he made a list of birds available in the Kumaon region. His list reads as follows ....

"(a) Birds that beautified nature's garden: In this group I put minivets, orioles and sunbirds.

(b) Birds that fill the garden with melody: thrushes, robins and shamas.

(c) Birds that regenerated the garden: barbets, hornbills and bulbuls.

(d) Birds that warned of danger: dronges, red jungle fowl and babblers.

(e) Birds that maintained the balance of nature: eagles, hawks and owls.

(f) Birds that performed the duty of scavangers: vultures, kites and crows."[23]

Corbett admitted that he got this knowledge not from any book but from the servants of his house and from the people like Kunwar Singh. Corbett, regardless of his immense knowledge of natural history, abhored snakes, and thought that snakes were dangerous, poisonous or harmless to him and he believed that killing a snake was auspicious for the immediate future. It was the traditional superstition of the forest people of Kumaon that Corbett straightaway imbibed. Corbett respected these people throughout his life and he wrote – "Those people. like Kunwar Singh knows the 'Jungle life' very well". [24] But Corbett never thought that these people were good hunters as well. While hunting was a pastime of the Maharajas and Europeans, it was a means of sustenance of the jungle people. Corbett ignored this basic fact about his forest friends.

Also, Jim's concept of hunting was typically European, for ever since his childhood he had believed that – "A hunter without a gun, however, is hardly a hunter at all". [25] He believed it throughout his life. Only the Europeans had guns, for big shooting. It was not possible for the common Indians to possess costly rifles. In his childhood he had the psychology that the forest people like Kunwar Singh or Harh Singh would locate the animals and he would shoot. Stephen Deuse presented him his first firearm, a double barreled, muzzle-loading shotgun. He regularly used this weapon to shoot birds. At the age of twelve, the Sergeant Major, who was in charge of the Cadets of his school, presented Jim a 450 Martini rifle. Jim shot many large animals with this powerful rifle. He derived his love for nature from the Indians, but the destructive penchant of a hunter from the Europeans.

Corbett joined the Bengal and North-Western Railway Company at the age of sixteen. He was sent to the forest of the Gangetic plains to organize the felling of trees for timber which were cut to specied size, as locomotive fuel, before being transported by the bullock cart to the nearest railway for collection.[26] The railways were the singlemost important factor responsible for massive destruction of the Indian forests.[27] It is ironical that Corbett, one of the first environmentalists of the present century, served the railways for long thirty years when his principal job was to destroy forests and supply timber to the railways. He organized every stage of the process whereby the trees were turned into timber of such size and variety as required by the railways.[28] To do all this he had a sizable work force under him. His treatment of the workers clearly showed that in spite of his Indian background he positively retained the typical superiority complex of the British coloniser Corbett, the so called 'almost Indian' never lost his racial identity.[29]

His allotted patch of forest was ten miles from the railway. There he set up his camp on the left bank of the Ganga near Bakhtiyarpur, twenty miles east of Patna where the Gandak river joined the main flow of the Ganga. For Corbett those days were pretty tough days and he mentioned it as 'hard days of life'.[30] He worked long hours in heat, regardless of the humidity of the monsoon or the scorchingly hot dry season. Corbett's description of these years of his life was similar to Kipling's description of his childhood days in India.

Kipling described these days as 'seven years hard' and expressed the fear of malaria and other tropical diseases in India.[31]

In these days, Corbett enjoyed night hunting in the Baktiyarpur forest where he killed cheetal, wild pig, the Indian four-horned antelope, forest hares and a wide variety of birds. He felled some five thousand cubic feet of timber. He cared over five hundred acres of forest land.[32] He had no confusion in destroying this large area of forest land because he regarded it as service to the British rule to which his loyalty remained unshaken. Corbett was not ignorant of the concepts like ecology, conservation and wildlife preservation from his childhood days. The British Government of India passed the first forest Act in 1865, and second forest Act in 1878, when Corbett was a child. From the 1860s, Forest Conservation became a major issue with the Government of India.[33] The Conservation policy of the Government took away all the traditional rights of the forest people. But the policy never checked the original hunting expeditions of the Maharajas and the Europeans and the felling of trees for the railway companies.[34] Although Corbett became an environmentalist in the later years, he could not feel the contradiction of the British Governmental policy. Corbett's childhood and nature of his first service in the railway companies exposed that it was very natural for Corbett to have this type of contradiction in his thinking about the Indian environment.

Jim Corbett participated in the environmental movements in the early decades of the twentieth century, particularly after retiring from the service of the railway company. He participated in the First World War and he was promoted to the post of Major of the Indian Army. He returned to India in the end of 1919. In the 1924s he began his movement for the protection of the environment. When the Bombay Natural History Society sought help to deal some environment related issues in 1927, Corbett assisted them in many ways.[35] He was the secretary of the 'Preservation of Wild Life Association in the United Provinces' in 1936-38.[36] He and Hasan Abid Jafri edited a journal entitled 'Indian Wild Life'.[37] The principal aim of the journal was to protect wildlife. From 'The Chital', the journal of the Wild Life Preservation Society of India, we know that Corbett was one of the leading activists in the wildlife preservation movement in the first half of the twentieth century. [38] Even when he settled in Africa after leaving India, he established a Wild Life Preservation Society there in 1949 and became it's secretary.[39] Even in the 'London Times' dated 10th May, 1955 we find that Corbett wrote a letter to Mr. Brambley, a well known preservationist and alerted about the possible disappearance of tiger from India.[40] From many other documents we find that Corbett was one of the main initiators of environmental movements in India.

Corbett's activities after the 1920s have been explained by many scholars like Martin Booth as activities after 'Gradual Realisation'.[41] We can also examine some events of Corbett's life from which nature of this realization may be clear. After First World War and Corbett's giving up of his contract with the railways, he settled permanently in Nainital to run his business with F.E.G. Mathews, Jim became one of the successful business men of Nainital by 1920 and also became the Vice-Chairman of the Municipal Board of Nainital in 1920.[42] In 1923, as the Chairman, he proposed the motion that the night fishing in the Naini Lake should be banned, in order to preserve the stocks. He was also intent on preserving the beauty of the town. Always aware of the flora and fauna of Nainital, he tried to get the whole town and it's environs declared as a bird sanctuary. Rules on the killing of the wild birds were drawn up earlier but rejected by the government. This sort of declaration was noco made legally void under the Wild Animals and Birds Protection Act of 1912. He purchased his first camera from 'Lawrie and his company' in 1912.[43] Slowly, according to Martin Booth, photography became his first choice and rifle became his second choice.[44] Jim was also unfigned by F.W. Champion, who was the pioneer of wild life photography in India. Champion was one of the first officer who was concerned not with flora but also with fauna.[45] Jim was so interested in photography that he came to Calcutta to purchase the latest model of 'Leise Model and Camera'. It was one of his first 35 mm cameras. Even Jim received a gift from Lord Strachcone a 'Bell and Howell' 16mm movie camera.[46] In August, 1932, Jim published an article entitled,

'Wild Life in the Village - An Appeal' in the 'Review of the Week' published from Nainital.[47] Jim Corbett, at this time, spoke to schools, colleges, hospitals, and church groups throughout the United Provinces to cultivate conservation awareness.[48] All these might at first suggest a change of attitude in the heart of Corbett in the post World War I period.

But a more critical approach shows a rather contrary picture. In 1920s, when he visited Tanganica for the first time, he and his friend Percy hunted a number of animals.[49] Tanganica had been declared a reserved forest by that time. Hunting was prohibited for the Africans, but not for the Europeans. The natives of Africa had little knowledge of cultivation. They had to depend on hunting. Wild beasts were killed to provide tribesmen with meat, leather or blood for drinking, Zebras were killed for leather than their decorative skins, antelopes were eaten. But initially no tribesman used to kill more animals than what they needed. Subsequently of course, they began to be engaged in hunting for commercial ends because of their poverty. The preservation policy deprived them of their traditional rights and ways of life. For economic reasons they joined as labourers in the railway companies in Africa. Railway tracks were expanded in Africa by this time.[50] Corbett's practical experience was started in the 'preserves' of Africa. But he did not have the ability to feel the limitations of the policy.

Corbett's activities in India exposed a similar contradiction. As the Vice-Chairman of the Nainital Municipality he tried to prevent night hunting in the Nainital Lake. At the same time, he arranged clearing of large forest areas of Choti Haldwani to extend farmlands.[51] He continued to organize tiger hunting for high European officials and Maharajas till the Second World War and in Africa he organized hunting for the British princes.[52] As the Chairman of Nainital Municipality he tried to expand the town areas and for this purpose felling of trees were absolutely necessary. He himself cleared forests to open more lands and sold those lands to other people. It was the same business of his father, Christopher William Corbett. Jim Corbett became a more successful businessman than his father. In 1938, Jim was one of these

Europeans who initiated the publicity for artificial urbanization and development documents which made the first move towards making Nainital a tourist attraction or a hill station.[53] Corbett was not conscious of such town planning. He restricted night fishing for the local people, but made different cemented platforms around Naini lake for providing fishing opportunities for the Europeans. They had to pay an amount of money to the municipality for using these platforms.

Corbett had a very close relation with the district officials, police officers and forest officials. He hunted with them and fished with them. He travelled many times throughout the Kumaon and Garwal region and if he could find out any illegal activities in the forest areas, he used to report it to the officers. But we find that he never gave any report against any European. The Public Works Committee, of which he was for some years the Chairman, was responsible for giving permission for the felling of trees within the town limits, which interestingly including some substantial forest tracts.[54] Until the end of the Second World War, Nainital lived under the influence of Corbett and his committed colleagues. Jim became very popular in Nainital. He was 'Major' Jim Corbett to the Europeans and 'Sahib' to the poor Indians.[55]

Photography never became Corbett's genuine hobby. We have enough evidence that he was mainly a hunter, and not a photographer even after 1930. One of his hunting trips was well documented by an army officer, Lionel Fortescue. Corbett accompanied by his faithful servant Moti Singh and Fortescue accompanied by his Indian servant James, made a shooting trip to Pangi and the Chenab valley. They hunted a number of animals. Although Corbett had his camera with him he rarely used to photograph the animals.[56] Lord Strachcone gifted a camera to Corbett. But it was actually in return of Corbett's help in the organized hunting of two tigers in the Kumaon forest area.[57] A personal studio was necessary to develop films in those days. Tim did not arrange his personal studio till 1938.[58]

The increasing interest of Jim in photography can be interpreted in a different way. From the 1930s, photography became increasingly a popular artistic medium in India. F.W. Champion, a pioneer of wildlife photography, wrote that it was more difficult to take a good photography of a wild animal than hunting it. [59] Champion was a forest officer and he had a very close relation with Corbett. Champion used to take photographs of wild animals and he sent these photographs to be printed in many newspapers and journals. Corbett also did the same. He wanted to be a good photographer as well as a good hunter. Taking photography and hunting wildlife did not appear to be contradictory to Jim Corbett. His interest in photography increased after 1940. But it does not mean that Corbett's interest in hunting expeditions decreased in this time. All the shikar expeditions of Jim Corbett prove that he retained his hunting habit till his death. So there was no stage of 'gradual realisation' as described by Martin Booth. He published his idea of environmental preservation and protection in many articles. But this idea was not different from the imperialist environmental policy of the British.

Corbett's imperialist bent of mind clearly emerges from a close analysis of his books. He wrote his first book 'Man-eaters of Kumaon' in 1946 which made a name for him. His second book 'Man-eating Leopard of Rudraprayag' was published in 1948. After that he wrote 'My India' in 1952, 'Jungle Lore' in 1953 and 'The Temple Tiger and More Man-eaters of Kumaon' in 1954. Besides these major books Corbett also wrote a number of articles. His last book was 'Tree Tops' which he finished thirteen days before his death on 10th April, 1955. These books reveal the environmental ideas of a mature mind.

From the writing of Jim Corbett it is very clear that he was very sympathetic to the Indians, especially those living in the forests and mountains. According to Corbett in 'My India', the India I know, where are four million people, ninety percent of whom are honest, brave, loyal, hard working souls whose daily prayer to God, and to whatever government is in power, is to give security to life and property to enable them to enjoy the fruits of their labour.' [60] Corbett was one of the few Europeans who tried to love the forest people as an insider, in his description of India. Corbett was sometimes nostalgic, even he sometimes analysed the customs and rituals of the Indians from an 'orientalist' point of view. But Corbett had no confusion that these 'brave, loyal' Indians should not rebel against the government in any situation and 'whatever government is in power.' Corbett himself was so loyal to the British Raj that in 1946 when his first book "Man-eaters of Kumaon" was published, the first response came from the British officials. The Viceroy Lord Linlithgow wrote Preface to the second edition of the book. Linlithgow and Corbett had enjoyed the game of "organised hunting" on a number of occasions. At this time when Corbett and Linlithgow killed four tigers in a single night. Five family members including three daughters of Lord Linlithgow participated in the hunting game in Kumaon. Corbett expressed much frustrations in his writing that he could not hunt the fifth tiger to satisfy the fifth member or the youngest daughter of Lord Linlithgow.[61] It was an incident of 1940s when Corbett had turned an environmentalist. Lord Linlithgow wrote in the Preface of Corbett's book – "During my stay in India I was in touch with many Europeans. I am sure that no European officer than Corbett knows the language of the forest so deeply."[62] In the Preface Linlithgow did not mention Corbett's love for forest, he narrated the story of 'organised hunting' which he enjoyed with Corbett many times. About the book Linlithgow explained – "Each and every one hunter should read this book before killing his first tiger".[63] Corbett's book emphasized the hunting of a man-eater. But Linlithgow emphasized the pleasure of killing a tiger, he did not mention the great amount of loss that was done by the man-eating tigers of Kumaon. Linlithgow introduced Corbett's book as "a tale well told of action and adventure."[64] Adventure in the mysterious world of Indian forests, according to Linlithgow was the main spirit of Corbett's book. It was white man's burden to explore the mystery. In the forest areas, where Corbett lived from his childhood was not practically mysterious land to Corbett, even Europeans completed their survey, listed all the plants and animals much before 1960s. But Linlithgow described the mystery of the land because 'mystery' always legitimized European intrusion in the forest lands of India. More than a hundred people were killed by the man-eater which Linlithgow did not mention. Even the man-eater itself was unfortunate enough to go into oblivion in the mind of the Viceroy.

M.G. Hallet compared Corbett's writing with Kipling's 'Jungle Book'. He said that Corbett wrote from his long experience and Kipling from his imagination. But according to Hallet there was no difference between Corbett and Kipling in the treatment of the forest. Kipling's idea of mystic forest is true and it can be proved by Corbett's experience. Hallet wrote – "Kipling's stories are facts, and fact is often stranger than fiction."[65] Like Linlithgow, Hallet went far from the main context of the book and described the courage of the Garwali soldiers. He observed – "These are the qualities which will be needed by our gallant soldiers as long as the war or Asia lasts against the human enemy of Tokyo who process in many respect the skill and power of the man-eater. This book, with it's fascinating description of village life, shows the highland villages, men, women and children. Their fighting men have shown the courage in many battlefields in Abyssinia, Libya and Malaya, and they will continue to show it till the power of Tokyo is destroyed." [66] In the book 'Man-eaters of Kumaon', Hallet ends his Introduction with such a statement which had no relation with Corbett's book. But the reflection of the ruler's psychology is there, and it is also exposed in Corbett's own writing.

Corbett believed in the infinite loyalty of the people of the forest. If we analyse his book 'My India', it seems to be very clear. Corbett wrote in the Dedication of this book – 'if you are looking for a history of India, you will not find it in these pages.[67] Corbett tried to write a new history which deal with the common people of India. He tried to give a new picture of India to the European readers. He wrote this book to 'My friends - the poors of India'.[68] Here the poverty of the people is highlighted not as a curse but as a 'magic-stick' of different qualities like courage, loyalty, honesty, simplicity etc. Corbett romanticized the poverty of the people. This sympathy was very much in tune with the 'highly civilized benevolent rulers'. When Corbett was a labour-officer of Mokhama Ghat in his service life, once the coolies of Mokhama Ghat did not get salary for a long period. But they were too loyal to be rebellious. Corbett in his book 'My India' tried to idealise their extreme loyalty. He wrote – 'Semistarvation had not impaired the loyalty of my men and they were willing to give battle to anyone'.[69] This was the favourite stand of the colonial government.

Corbett described Henry Ramsay, the Commissioner of Nainital, as the 'King of Kumaon'.[70] He glorified the judgement of Ramsay – 'In no case was his judgment known to be questioned, nor did any man who he had sentenced to a fine or imprisonment fail to pay the fine or imprisonment or fail to pay the fine into the Government treasury or fail to report himself at the nearest jail to carry out the term of simple or rigorous imprisonment which Ramsay had sentenced him.'[71] Corbett established both the supremacy of the ruler and the duality of the subjects in this passage. Corbett fully shared the patronizing mentality of the colonial master.

From the passages it is clear that Corbett was conscious of this distance from the Indians. That he never really identified himself with Indians is clearly proved by his departure from India, his land of birth in the closing years of his life. He sometimes romanticized his ideas to overcome this distance. The style of writing of 'My India' was just like that of a tourist who described his close affinity with the Indians from a detached point of view, in other words, without a real sense of belonging. Corbett wrote – 'Pick up cape comorin the most south point of the Peninsula, and run your eye straight up to where the Gangetic plane slopes up into the foothill of the Himalayas in the north of the united provinces, there you will find the hill station of Nainital.' [72] This style was more like that of a tourist guide guiding his reader to know many natural aspects of India. Corbett's self identity as a European is very clear. The common people described Corbett as 'Sahib', 'Gora Sadhu' etc. Corbett thought that these people are a part of nature and they are as simple as the other objects of nature. His naturopathy itself had a colonial gaze. He did not recognize any right of the common Indian workers. He, in the other way, idealized the entire system – 'There were no trade unions or slaves and slave drivers in those days and every individual was at liberty to work as many or as few hours as he or she wished to, and everyone worked carefully and happily.'[73]

Corbett believed in an infinite peace in the forest which is clear from his writing in 'The Laws of the Jungles'. At the end of the passage he wrote – 'Three of the greatest men in the British Empire, wrote condemning war atrocities, and accusing the enemy of attempting to introduce the 'law of the jungle' into the dealing of warring man and man. Had the creator made for the jungle folk, there would be no wars.'[74] Corbett never supported any rebellion of the people. In the 1930s when the 'Jungle Satyagraha' was fired up on the entire Garwal and partly Kumaon region Corbett was not only present there physically, but he was also the Chairman of Nainital Municipality at the time. But he was totally silent about this movement.[75]

The original inhabitants of the mountain could not accept the European intrusion without resistance. The resistance in Kumaon were sometimes active and most of the time passive. Corbett mentioned in 'My India' a story which he heard in his childhood – " .... hill people were unwilling to disclose the position of their sacred lake. One of these administrators, in the year 1839, hit upon the ingenious plan of placing a large stone on the head of a hill man, telling him he would have to carry it until he arrived at Goddess Naini's lake. After wandering over the hills for many days the man eventually got tired of carrying the stone, that led the party who was following him to the lake."[76] This was a self-made rumour spread by European residents of Nainital. It was a story of European intrusion and resistance of the common people. But Corbett described it as the story of a romantic adventure to find out a new world.

Corbett's support to the governmental policy of identifying one tribal group as 'Criminal tribes' also exposed his psychology. The 'Bhantus' were one of the so-called criminal tribes. Corbett wrote – 'The Government gave rent-free land to these people, but they did not change their character.'[77] Corbett helped the police to find out Sultana, the leader of the Bhantus in the remote forest area. Corbett described Sultana as 'India's Robin Hood'.[78] He wrote about the escape of Sultana in a very detouched manner – 'with the rights and wrongs of classifying a tribe as 'criminal' and confining it within the four walls of Najibad Fort, I am not concerned. It suffices to say that Sultana, with his young wife and infant son escaped from the fort.'[79] Corbett almost made an expedition with Freddy Young of the police force to find out Sultana. The description of this expedition by Corbett in 'My India' is not different from that of the expedition to find out a man-eater in the forest. He romanticized Sultana as 'India's Robin Hood'. He admitted that 'Sultana had helped the poor in many ways, he did not refuse any beggar and he never took anything from the poor' [80] Sultana was important to Corbett not for his rights, but for his strength and vigour.

Corbett served the British Raj in many ways. He himself willingly joined the First World War and promoted to the post of Major. He trained the soldiers in guerilla warfare at the time of the Second World War. His long experience in Indian forests helped him in this service, and he was promoted to the post of Lieutenant Colonel this time. In 1946 he was honoured by the British Government as 'Friend of the Indian Empire' for his distinguished service to the Raj.

Corbett had his extreme loyalty to the British royal family. When Corbett was settled in Africa after leaving India, the Duke of Edinburgh and Princess Elizabeth went there. Corbett had the opportunity to spend few hours with the Duke and the Princess. Corbett wrote a small book named 'Tree Tops' to describe his unique experience with the Princess. Corbett romantically described – 'In my long life, I have seen many courageous people. But what I have seen on the fifth day of February cannot be compared with any previous experience. The Princess and her companions were so eager to visit the tree tops that they ignored the danger of the wild elephants in this remote forest of Africa.[81] But practically what the Princess and the Duke did was nothing. They only watched the animals from a long distance. Corbett mentioned it as their 'extreme bravery'. He was so moved that he wrote – 'I shall keep this memory alive till the last moment of my life.'[82] This was an example of Jim's loyalty to the British Raj till the last days of his life. He died just thirteen days after writing this small book 'Tree Tops'.

Corbett's contradictions are very clearly exposed. Even now in the place of Jhind, there are five tanned skins of tigers and it is written in the side of the tanned skins – 'Jim's Tiger'. Corbett killed a number of tigers to satisfy the King of Jhind. Inspite of all criticism, Corbett had some definite contribution in the early environmental movement in India. There were many approaches in the nineteenth and twentieth centuries.

The most important concept of the environmental movement of the world was the concept of 'Scientific Preservation'. But most of the colonial government, including the British Government in India never took this scientific approach in preserving environment. They only emphasised on the ethical approaches of environmental preservation where preserving of unique species of the world is the single important factor. Preservation of tiger was important in this ethical approach, but there is no bar on the destruction of forest by felling trees. These ideas of 'deep ecology' as described by Ramachandra Guha helped the process of destruction. Jim Corbett was also influenced by this idea. So he had no confusion of destroying a large area of forests. He only thought of preserving the animals of forests in the last decades of his life. But as a European, he was never against the hunting games of the Maharajas and the Europeans.

It is true that Corbett was unconsciously guided by the negative aspects of the colonial environmental policy. His love for nature and his sympathy towards the common people of India was to a great extent genuine. It can't be explained simply by the theories of imperialism. Corbett was definitely an environmentalist and also a humanist of the time. But both his environmental ideas and his humanism were influenced and dominated by the British colonial ideology. Corbett was one of the very few Europeans from whom we can find a very definite colonial perspective on the environmental history of India.

Notes and References

1 Martin Booth, 1986, *Carpet Sahib*, p. 7, OUP, New Delhi.

2. Ibid., p. 31.
3. Stowell, V.A., 1907, *A Manual of the land Tenures of the Kumaon District*, p. 237, Allahabad.
4. Jalecl. Jerry A, 1997, *Under the shadow of' Man-eaters,* p. 18-29, for early days, New Delhi.
5. See Madhav Gadgil and Ramachandra Guha, 1992 edited *The Fissured Land*, p. 118, OUP, New Delhi.
6. Batten, J. H., 1878, *Official Reports of the Settlement in Kumaon*, Calcutta.
7. Walton, H.G., 1911, *Kumaon - A Gazetteer*, p. 173, Allahabad.
8. Booth, Op. cit., p. 33.
9. Walton, op. cit., p. 177.
10. Batten, op. cit., p. 221.
11. Booth, op. cit., p. 35.
12. Ibid, p. 38.
13. Ibid, pp. 40-42.
14. Ibid, p. 46.
15. Ibid, p. 30.
16. Jim Corbett, 1952, *My India*, p. 17-18 (Third Edition, 1980, OUP, Delhi).
17. Pant, G. B., 1922, *The Forest problems in Kumaon*, p. 118, Allahabad.
18. Ibid, p. 23.
19. Corbett, op. cit., p. 18.
20. Ibid, p. 21.
21. Booth, op. cit., p. 39.
22. Corbett, op. cit., p. 5.
23. Booth, op. cit., p. 47.
24. Corbett, op. cit., p. 18.
25. Booth, op. cit., p. 50.
26. Kala, D.C., 1979, *Jim Corbett of Kumaon,* p. 36-45, Ravi Day, Delhi.
27. See Avon's *History of Indian Railways*, (Delhi, 1964) where he described in details the early activities of the Railway companies.
28. Guha & Gadgi, op. cit., p. 118.
29. Booth, op. cit., p. 63.
30. Corbett, op. cit., p. 177.
31. Kipling Rudyard, 1957, *Something on myself'*, p. 9, England.

32. Booth, op. cit., p. 82.
33. D. Brandis, 1884, *Progress of Forestry in India*, Edinburg. (See the Introduction of Brandis. He initiated conservation in India in 1864-77).
34. Ranganathan Mahesh, 1993, *Fencing the Forest*, p. 27, OUP, Delhi.
35. Mahasweta Devi, 1993 ed., *Complete Works of Jim Corbett*, (In Bengali), p. 25, Kolkata.
36. Booth, op. cit., p. 214.
37. Ibid, p. 215.
38. See *The Chetal*, journal of Wild Life Preservation Society of India, 1958, Dehradun.
39. Booth, op. cit., p. 221.
40. London Times, 10th May, 1955.
41. Booth, op. cit., p. 157.
42. We find detailed reports of Corbett's activities from the titles of Nainital Municipality from 1920-37.
43. Jim Corbett, 1954, *Man-eaters of Kumaon*, p. 72, Delhi. (He explained his growing interest of photography in this part of the book).
44. Booth, op. cit., p. 165.
45. See souvenir of Forest Research Institute, Dehradun, entitled *Hundred Years of Indian Forestry*, published in 1965. (Detailed account of F.W. Champion as a forest officer and photographer).
46. Booth, op. cit., p 167.
47. *Review of the Week*, Nainital, This article appeared in Vol I, No. 2 *Indian Wild Life*, Dehradun, 1936.
48. Booth, op. cit., pp. 184-185.
49. Ibid, p. 235.
50. Kjeskshus, H, 1977, *Ecology control and economic development in East African History*, University of California Press, Berkeley.
51. Booth, op. cit., p. 161.
52. Jim Corbett, 1957, *Tree Tops*, p. 8, England.
53. Booth, op. cit., p. 172.
54. Ibid, p. 177.
55. Corbett, My *India*, op. cit., p. 3.
56. Corbett, *Maneaters of Kumaon*, op. cit., pp. 74-75.
57. Ibid, p. 76.

58. Booth, op. cit., p. 171.
59. Champion, *Memoirs*, *Hundreds Years of Forestry*, op. cit., p. 112.
60. Jim Corbett, *My India*, op. cit., p. 1.
61. Jim Corbett, 1953, *Jungle Lore*, p. 27, England.
62. Corbett, *Maneaters of Kumaon*, p. 1.
63. Ibid, p. 2.
64. Ibid, p. 2.
65. Ibid, p. 3.
66. Ibid, p. 4.
67. Jim Corbett, *My India*, op. cit.
68. Ibid, p. 5.
69. Ibid, p. 48.
70. Ibid, p. 60.
71. Ibid, p. 61.
72. Ibid, p. 5.
73. Ibid, p. 142.
74. Ibid, p. 77.
75. For Forest Satyagraha of 1930 see article by D.E.V. Baker, *A Serious Time*, in *Indian Economic and Social History Review*, Vol. 21, No. 21, 1984.
76. Jim Corbett, op. cit., p. 7.
77. Ibid, p. 90.
78. Ibid, p. 90.
79. Ibid, p. 91.
80. Ibid, p. 93.
81. Jim Corbett, "Tree Tops" op. cit., p. 10.
82. Ibid, p. 12.

4

Declining Flora and Fauna of Frontier Bengal (1870 – 1930)

Anindita Majumdar

The forest areas of the western Bengal in the Civil Division of Burdwan, Bankura, Birbhum, Midnapore and Purulia were distributed roughly in an isosceles triangle. The forests were chiefly located in the lateritic belt, through which ran the principal rivers, Brahmani, Mayurakshi, Ajay, Damodar, Dwarakeswar and Kangsabati into the Hooghly while Subarnarekha, the southern most river drained independently into the Bay of Bengal. The forests consisted predominantly of a thick belt of sal in the lateritic areas as well as in most other parts of the tract (the hills). On the typical Chota Nagpur formations mostly in Purulia and parts of Bankura miscellaneous species occurred to the exclusion of Sal, like *Dalbergia latifolia, Ougenia dalbergoides, Boswellia serrata, Sterculia urens, and sometimes the bamboo Dendrocalamus strictus.* [1]

At the dawn of history part of the tract appears to have been included in the country known as "Radha and Vajravumi". The eastern part of the district with its level soil formed part of "Radha" while the more rugged portion to the west was called the "Vajravumi", [2] i.e., the country of the thunderbolt. A graphic description of this tract is given in Acaranga Sutra, one of the oldest Jain Scriptures. Another earlier historical reference is to be found in the Bhabhishyat Purana compiled in 15-16th century A.D. It spoke of Varahabhumi, Samantabhumi and Manbhumi which were overspread with impenetrable forests of Sal and other trees. [3] We find that upto the greater part of the sixteenth century the Pathans held these territories. In the Mughal period the Northern portion i.e. Dumka, Birbhum etc. of this tract was known as Damin-i-koh and the hilly jungle portion as Jharkhand. The Marathas swept this tract in course of their raids in the middle of the 18th century for two decades and finally the tract came under the British in 1760. At that time Burdwan comprised besides the present district, the whole of Bankura, formerly known as western Burdwan, together with Birbhum and Hooghly. In 1805 all these territories were made into a new district called the "Jungle Mahals". The formation and changes of the contours are important because the land-tenures and forests of the so called 'Jungle Mahals' overlapped each other to a large extent. The forces of Permanent Settlement with increasing revenue demand, the introduction of railways making the woodlands more profitable, granting of ijaras to Midnapore Zamindari Company, Watson and Company, played decisive roles in the decrease of forest cover in these private forested zones.

Burdwan district was covered by alluvium except in the Asansol subdivision where Gondwana rocks were exposed. The soii was partly a lateritic clay. [4] J.C.K. Peterson mentioned that "there are no forests properly so called in the district but a large tract of about hundred square miles in the Ausgram police station, and the western uplands of the Asansol subdivision are covered with young Sal (*shorea robusta*)". [5] The forests did not yield much revenue and no trees of any size were found. They were cut down when the railway was under construction. But attention was drawn to their value and some of them were closely preserved. The sal saplings were chiefly used as rafters and beams and had a special value for this purpose on account of their immunity from the attacks of white ants.[6] In the Settlement Report of Burdwan by K.A.L. Hill (Final Report on the Survey and Settlement Operations in the District of Burdwan between 1927-1934, the area of Burdwan was shown to be 2701 square miles. The Ishaque Report of 1944-45 showed 801,505 acres under forests. The picture coming out shows that the utilisation of the forests of this belt was for minor purposes. On 23rd January 1939, some forests of the Burdwan Raj at Patharmara and Sonamukhi were inspected by the Forest Committee appointed by the Government of Bengal. The tour brought out the fact that the forests of south-western Bengal of Burdwan, Bankura, Birbhum and Midnapore were vanishing and that the soil was being denuded in the district. Throughout the Report the desiccationist trends of soil erosion denuding the forest cover, and the danger of West Bengal becoming more liable to flood and drought were stressed upon.[7]

The greater portion of Bankura consisted of laterite and alluvium while metamorphic or gneissose rocks were found to the extreme west.[8] A detailed picture of the flora of the district reveals that the district contained wild deep forests which were found in a denuded condition in the year 1939. Scant remains of the forests were found by the Committee near Susunia, Saltore, Jhantipahari, Basudebpur in the Vishnupur subdivision, Maliara Estate at Latiaboni and of tenure holders near Gangajalghati. The northern central and south eastern uplands of the district contained isolated pockets of dense forests of Sal (shorea robusta) while the surrounding low hills were covered by a mixed forest containing species of *Miliusa, Schleichera, Diospyros* and other trees. The uplands were covered with scrub jungle of zizyphus and other thorny shrubs.[9] The open forests in the eastern and south-eastern part contained trees typical of the eastern sub-Himalayan range like the valuable Asan tree (*Terminalia tomentosa*), red cotton tree (*Bombax malabaricum*). Asan yielded high quality wood used for making lintels and door posts.[10] The leaves provided one of the main supplies of food to the tusser silkworm. The more characteristic species that were found were Glycosmis, Polyalthia, Suberosa, Clerodenaron infortunatum, Solanum torvum and various other species of figs in particular, the pipal and banyan, mango (*Mangifera indica*) and Jiyal (odina wodier). Moreover there were also *Wendlandia exserta, Gmelina arborea, Adina cordifolia, Holarrhena antidysenterica, Wrightia tomentosa, Vitex Negundo and Stephegyne parvifolia.* [11]

To name a few of the most common trees that were of economic and medicinal values included Alkushi (Mucuna Pruriens), used as a blister, Amaltas used as laxative, Babul as medicine, Bair (Zizyphus Jujuba) used for fencing, Bel (Aegle Marmelos) utilised in dysenteric and heart diseases, bag bherenda (Jatropha Curcas) used as cathartic. Over and above Bichuti (Tragia involucrata), Bahera (Terminalia belerica), Dhatura (Datura stramonium), Gab (Diospyros Embryopteris), Harva, Imli, Kuchila, Mahua, Palas, Sajina, Kend etc. which served multifarious purposes.[12] In Bankura large supplies of lac and tasar were available which were gathered by Santals and Bauris.

As to the fauna wild elephants, leopards, bears were found in plenty in the extensive sal jungles; and at Saltora jungles in the north-west, tiger was occasionally seen. But as early as 1908 O'Malley reported that the district was far from being well stocked with game. This according to him was "due to the gradual thinning out and entire extermination of the extensive sal jungles which once covered the uplands and the continued extension of cultivation which have gradually driven big game westwards.:"[13] The Settlement Report of Bankura by F.W. Robertson reported between 1917-24 "The greatest change which has come over this district during the past half century has been cutting down of forests. In other districts deforestation usually connotes increase in cultivation and a general rise in the economic condition of the people. In Bankura no such fortunate results have been obtained. Although everywhere increase in land under cultivation is apparent, the district is not supporting a larger population. In the Sadar Division there has been cutting down of jungles."[14] In the Settlement Report of Bankura the total area under jungles was shown to be 332,967.15 acres.

The Ishaque Report[15] concerning Bankura reported 219,710.62 acres under forests and 41,512.71 acres under jungles.

By 'Forests' the Report said it meant areas covered by sal jungles. The sal forest covered an area of 219,710.62 acres. The Report commented that an extensive sal forests were of great economic benefit to the district which help in catching rains, getting fuel and cowdung. Thus there was considerable decrease in the area covered by jungles since Settlement operations. The Report asserted that the indiscriminate destruction of sal forest was a menace to agriculture, affecting rainfall leading to drought and "their proper maintenance under supervision of the Government is a standing necessity."[16]

The very word Birbhum, Bir in Mundari language meaning jungle and Bhumi meaning land, meant "Jungle land". In "Brahma Khanda" section of "Bhavishva Purana" a work probably composed in 15th or 16th century it is referred to for the first time as "Birbhumi" as "three-fourth of the district are jungle."[17] It formed a part of the eastern fringe of the Chotanagpore plateau and oldest metamorphic rocks, the Gondwana system, laterite and gangetic alluvium went to the formation of the Birbhum district.[18] The country was more or less covered with dense forests having numerous hill and jungle passes guarded by the ghatwals or the ghat police, and only one-third of the total district was under cultivation.[19] The two main rivers are Ajai and Mayurakshi. River flows through the centre of the district from west to east. The other important rivers are Hingla, Sal (Kopai), Brahmani and Dwarka. Remains of forest were found in the western part adjoining the hills of Jharkhand (previous Santal Parganas). Near the western boundary were found high ridges of laterite separated by valleys. The larger ridges were covered with thick but stunted sal (Shorea robusta), piar (Buchanania latifolia), dhan (Anogeissus latifolia), kend (Diospyros melanoxylan) and mahua (bassia latifolia).[20] In 1863 J.E. Gastrell remarked "unrestricted clearing of the jungles has had great influence in decreasing the annual amount of rain and impoverishing the country. What half a century ago was thick jungle and waving plains of grass is now almost a sterile and barren waste."[21]

The western part of the jungle was an important source of minor forest produce of the district. O'Malley reported that there were land reserved for the growth of sal trees called "Jangal Bhumi". The trees were sold standing, as well as after being cut.[22] A large number of trees were also cut when young and sold for fuel. Silk and lac were important forest produce of the district. The manufacture of silk was the principal industry of Birbhum. Tusser was another marketable product of the district. Cocoons were gathered from the forest trees by aboriginal or semi aboriginal tribes. To meet the demand, the weavers got their supply also from Santal Parganas (Jharkhand). Lac manufacture was another important industry. It was an important forest product obtained from twigs of the Kusum trees. The raw material consisted of resinous gum round the dead bodies of the insects (Cocus lacca) buried in the gum formed on the twigs. [23]

Thus in a variety of ways the lives of the inhabitants were intimately dependent on the products of the woodlands. In the eastern portion of the district species of Aponogeton, Utricularia, Droseva, Dopatrium, Ilysanthes, Hydrolea Sphenoclea and similar aquatic plants were found in abundance. The western part of the district was comparatively dry and undulating, where species of Wendlandia, Evolvulus, Stipa, Tragus, Perotis, Spermacoce, Zizyphus, Capparis and other similar plants along with mango, palm, bamboo and other trees including jack and terminalia arjuna were present. [24] Writing in the mid 1850 Sherwill noted that nearly 20% of the population of Birbhum was involved in tussar silk collection, processing, weaving or marketing. [25] By the early 1970 the weaving industry had declined significantly in part due to the need to import cocoons which had been available in abundance in the area in the past.

As to the fauna of the district the carnivora consisted of leopards, bears, wolves and other small species. The Birbhoom jungles provided shelter to thieves and were also infested with wild snakes and tigers and elephants. The Raja of Birbhum admitted in a parwana (order) in 1775 that "Taluk Mullah and other twenty nine mouzhas in Tappeh kurrea have been dissolved by the ravages of robbers and tigers."[26] In the late 1780 at least fifty six villages were destroyed because of the depredations of wild elephants.[27] The Collector of Birbhum wrote in August, 1787 that the mischief of wild elephants might overrun the whole district. Wolves, wild pigs were found in isolated tracts of the jungle.[28] The district authorities took measures to counter the menace of the wild beasts of Birbhum. It seemed that the Government measures against the wild elephants achieved success, for in the fauna list by Captain Sherwill in 1852, reported that elephant was conspicuous by its absence. W.W. Hunter writing in 1860 remarked that "it is now impossible to find an undomesticated elephant and very rarely possible to hear of a tiger throughout the length and breadth of the district. The last tiger-hunt took place in May 1864."[29] He moreover commented that the tiger or leopard hunt was once the pastime and profit of the Santals of Birbhum.[30] O'Malley in 1910 gave a vivid description of the fauna of the woodlands which definitely showed a drastic decrease in their number.[31] "Leopards are not numerous, found chiefly in the Chaupahari jungle and Charicha jungle; bears are very rare sometimes only visit from hills of Santal Parganas to west of Rajnagar; wolves are sometimes met with in small patches; wild pigs in isolated tracts mostly killed by Santals during their great annual hunts."[32]

The forests were not in a much elevated position too. The Settlement Report of Birbhum showed that the area of cultivation increased greatly during last half century by Santals who reclaimed large tracts of jungles in the west of the district. They appeared to have migrated towards the close of the 18th century being brought in (and this is important) to clear the jungle and drive out wild beasts.[33] On 23rd Jan, 1939 forests of Birbhum were inspected by the Forest Committee.[34] It is much lamentable that the impenetrable jungles infested with tigers and elephants reached a dilapidated condition just by the turn of the 20th century. In 1944-45 the Ishaque Report showed that most of the forests had been cleared up by then. It reported forest area of Suri at 13,597.11 acres and that of Rampurhat subdivision at 813.31.[35]

The characteristic formation of Midnapore district is mostly laterite in north and west but in the south and east are found ordinary alluvium. The lateritic west "possesses a flora closely approximating to that of Chota Nagpur in which some parts are entirely waste, while other parts contain jungles of small sal, kusum and piasal and piasal yields a valuable wood and is fairly abundant."[36] The eastern tract which formed an extension of the rice swamp of Central Bengal, the vegetation was almost entirely aquatic, and species of Sagittaria, Aponogeton, Potamogeton, Butomopsis, Utricularia, Vallisneria Stratiotes, Nymphoea were abundant. Towards the south-east the conditions resembled those of the savannah swamps of the Sundarbans, the principal species being nal grass (Phragmites Karka). The western part of the district was largely covered with jungle of Shorea robusta (sal) or of a mixed forest, in which species of Aglaia, Schleichera, Schrebera, Terminalia and similar trees and climbers were present. Moreover there were also sprinkles of Ficus, Bassia, Butea, Tamarind etc. [37]

Practically the entire forest tract had a pure coppice of Shorea robusta. There were Madhuca latifolia, Pterocarpub marsupium, Diospyros melanoxylon, Terminalia tomentosa, Terminalia belerica, Lagerstroemea parviflora, Buchanania latifolia, Semecarpus anacardium, Careya arborea, Adina cordifolia, Aegle marmelos, Anogeissus latifolia, Streblus asper, Bridelia retusa, Butea frondosa, Salmalia malabarica, Eugenia spp, Dillenia pentagyna, Lanneagrandis, Grewia spp, Schleichera trijuga, Soymidafebrifuga, Embelia robusta, Ixora parviflora etc. 38 Undergrowth consisted of Cleistanthus collinus, Holarrhena antidysenterica, Gardenia gummifera, Gardenia turgida, Croton oblongifolius, Flacourtia spp, Combretum decandrum, Zizyphus jujuba, Zizyphus xylopyrus, Urena repunda, Lantana camara etc. Herbs consisted of Asparagus racemosus, Hemedesurus indicus etc. and grasses Aristida Chrysopogon, Desmostachya also occurred. Neighbouring to densely populated areas there are 'jhanti jungle' consisting of shorea robusta, Holarrhena antidysenterica, Diospyros melanoxylon etc. These were the remnants of old Sal coppice.

There were no reserved or protected forests in the district but there were several unclassed forests within the permanently settled estates.[39] These forests consisted mainly of small sal, "the trees being generally cut down when only eight or nine years old and exported to Calcutta for building purposes."[40] Other trees which were common in these forests were Mahua (Bassia latifolia), the tamarind and Palas (Butea frondosa), besides Kusum and piasal. The jungle products consisted of lac, tussar, cocoons, wax, resin, dhatura, firewood and various jungle roots. Among cthers were hogla rush used for making mats and for thatching, sola and cyperus segetinus a sedge used for making the mats for which Midnapore was famous.[41]

The Settlement Report of Midnapore[42] noted in 1917 that "The decrease in the cultivated area is the most surprising feature," that is forest lands were reclaimed for agriculture. The desiccationist note as "Soil deprived of the binding force of tree roots tends to get washed from the slopes into the valley by torrential rains" was also noticed in the Report. Thus large portions of forests were ravaged. The Forest Committee of 1939 visited between 4th-13th January the forests of Midnapore[43] and the area of inspection, brings to light even to a layman, the extensive forest areas of Midnapore that were deforested. The forests they visited included the forests of the Midnapore Zamindari Company at Amlagora and Goaltor, Lalgarh and Ramgarh Estate in Midnapore sadar subdivision, Jhargram Estate forests at Rakhgerya, Bandi, Goradhara and Arjun. Moreover forests of Belpahari, Midnapore Zamindari Company's forests at Lachmanpur and Sinduria hills were also inspected. Jamboni Estate forests at Chichira and Mayurbhanj state forests at Nayabasan which were in Jhargram subdivision were also inspected. "Vanishing forests" was the landscape that they were forced to see. The Ishaque Report of 1944-45[44] brought to light that sal forests covered an area of only 266,072.43 acres.

The carnivora of Midnapore were represented by tiger, leopard, bear, hyaena, fox, jackals etc. If the account of the fauna of the district given by L.S.S. O'Malley in his Gazetteer were taken to be a fair estimate of the presence of wild animals one is struck by the amazingly fast rate at which they dwindled in forty years. The reasons mainly were frequent cuttings of sal coppice forests which were not given the chance to grow more than 15' to 20' high on an average over most parts of the district, sometimes due to Santal hunt and sometimes by shikar expeditions. O'Malley reported as early as 1911 that wild elephants were occasionally seen, and larger carnivora were found only in the western part of the district where the most part was covered with sal jungle. O'Malley's account reveals that the annals of old Calcutta Tent Club contained references to the sport obtained in Tamluk and old cultivators mentioned name of Lord Mayo as having visited the place for sport.[45] Tigers once plentiful were very rare though bears and leopards were still plentiful. Purulia district owes its name to an ordinary village which had gradually grown in importance and became the headquarters of the erstwhile Manbhum district in 1838. The name was retained when Puruliya was separated from Bihar and joined to West Bengal in 1956.[46]

The tracing of forests, land forms and legislations, thereby of this district are deciphered mainly from Survey and Settlement Report of the district of Manbhum and Bengal District Gazetteers. Manbhum, as Puruliya came into existence in the year 1956. To cut a long story short and to make the forest graph and legislations pertaining to it clearer, an attempt has been made in the paragraphs below. Our earliest glimpse into this buffer zone gives very scant information about Purulia before the East India Company obtained the Diwani of Bengal, Bihar and Orissa in 1765. Purulia formed the eastern fringe of the inaccessible country of the Vajra-bhumi and was one of sixteen Mahajanapads of eastern India mentioned in the Jaina Bhagavati-sutra of 5th century A.D.[47] The aborigines of the greater portion of the district were mainly made up of Kurmi, Santal, Bhumij, Bauri, Kora, Mahli and Munda et al.[48] Most probably Puruliya formed a part of the mighty kingdoms of Sasanka, Palas, Senas in the 7th century, as also the Mughals.

The study of "Jungle Mahals" shows that this particular tract proved problematic as the revenues of this area were not accruing to the company. The reason being the area was intractable and the zamindars and chiefs could avoid revenue by hiding in the remote jungle areas. Among those chiefs there were the Rajas of Barabhum, Manbhum and Ramgarh. This was a troublesome estate and by Regulation XVIII of 1805, a 'Jungle Mahal' district; including the present Purulia district, parts of Birbhum, Bardhaman, Bankura and Midnapore was formed.[49] During the twenty five years succeeding the formation of the `Jungle Mahals' district, the area was brought under much closer control. By Regulation XIII of 1833[50] the district of the "Jungle Mahals" was broken and a new district called Manbhum was constituted. Manbhum at that time included a large part of Bankura and Burdwan as well. In 1838 the headquarters of Manbhum district was removed to 'Purulia' described then as lying 'in the centre of the jungles'[51] and formed part of SWFA (South West Frontier Agent). The districts enmeshed in such a manner make compartmentalisation of their profile difficult. In 1869 Valentile Ball[52] gave a list of the trees of Manbhum. By 1910 Coupland reported that four sections into which Mr. V. Ball divided the district the first, that is "original jungle land in which trees are of large size," has almost entirely disappeared.[53] The second, stunted jungle land from which timber was regularly cut and where the trees were never allowed to attain respectable dimension, was described as the bulk of jungle that survived.[54] The most characteristic trees of the first division given by Ball as early as 1869 included Sal, Asan, Kusum, Kend and Piar.[55] Dr. A. Campbell[56] of Pokhuria gave a list of trees and plants most important in the area which yielded good timber. They included Dilleniaceoe, species of the genus Dillenia, Capparidaceoe Caparis horrida, Ampelideoe, Anacardiaceoe (Odina Wodier) Leguminosae, Sapotaceoe - Bassia latifolia, Ebenaceoe - species of Diospyros, Urticaceoe, Gramineoe etc. A few significant patches of laterite marked the eastern most parts of the Purulia district. The allivium could be found in the western borders. It was a part of the 'Jungle Mahals' a land of tropical moist deciduous forests characterised by lofty trees rising to forty metres to form the top canopy. This has now degraded to tropical dry deciduous forests due to biotic interference such as shifting cultivation fire grazing and also unscientific forest management.[57]

Coming back to Manbhum which was part of lower Chotonagpore we find it was situated on the east of Lohardagga and Hazaribagh district. It was formed of low swelling ridges with isolated hills scattered over them. Fed by Subarnarekha, deposits of coal were found in huge quantities. As early as 1873 W. Schlich[58] as Conservator of Forests, Bengal, examined the forests of Chotonagpore. The Report stated that little information was available regarding the Manbhum Forests.[59] The Report confirmed however that Manbhum formed a part of vast sea of sal forests of Chotonagpore. Lower mixed forests was seen in Manbhum, containing large proportion of Acacia Catechu, Terminalia tomentosa, Butea frondosa,. Zizyphus jujuba and others.[60] Extensive forests existed along the boundary of Manbhum.[61] The common herbs, shrubs and trees of the Manbhum division contained large gregarious sal or shorea robusta. There were also Ach (Morinda tinctoria), Alkosi (Mucuna prurita) Am (Mangifera indica) Amla (Emblica officinalis) Ankol (Alangium Lemarckii), Arar (Acacia pennata), Arjun (Terminalia arjuna) Asan (Terminalia tomentosa), Baberang (Emblica robusta), Bair (Zizyphus jujuba), Bans (Dendrocalamus strictus), Bar (Ficus bengalensis) Belonjan (Cordia macleodii), Bhelwa (Semecarpus anacardium), Pisal (Peterocarpus marsupium), Bis tendu (Diospyros montana), Chakora (Milchelia champaca), Chatavan (Alstonia Scholaris), Chireta (Swertia pulchella), Churchu (Casearia tomentosa), Dathora (Zizyphus oenoplia), Dhawai (Woodforlia fruticosa) Dhaura (Anogeissus latifolia), Datranga (Ethretia laevis), Gaj (Millettia auriculata), Gamhar (Gmelina arborea), Harsinghar (Nyctanthes arbortristis), Jamun (Eugenia jambolana), Kadam (Anthocephalus cadamba), Kaim (Mitragyna purviflora), Kamjni (Murraya exotica), Kari (Miliusa velutina), Katahi (Flacourtia Ramontchii), Kessai (Bridelia retusa), Kurchi (Holarrhoena antidysenterica), Kusum (Schlei chera trijuga), Mainphal (Randia dumetorum), Maula (Buted parviflora), Nim (Azadirachta indica), palas (Butea frondosa), Perar (Randia uliginosa), Pipal (Ficus religiosa), Putus (Lantana camara), Ratangurur (Elaeodendron glaucum, Sabai (Eulaliopsis binata), Sandan (Ougeinia dalbergioides}; Siris (Albizzia stipulata), Sisso (Dalbergia sisso), Toon (Cedrela toona), Thingari (Lannea grandis)[62] etc. Over and above these Mahul and Haritaki jungles existed.[63] Lac was extensively grown on kul, kusum, palas, babla, pakur, dumur, pipal, kariar, satsal, lipsi and sisu trees.[64] Tusser was reared in Chas and Tundi areas.[65] The Settlement Report recorded an area of 781 square miles of jungles within the district.[66]

In Manbhum the forests were all zamindaris though many of them were seriously deforested by the demands of railway and public works department. The Bengal Nagpore Railway which passed through Manbhum, whose length in Bengal was two hundred miles, required 400,000 broad gauge sleepers besides considerable quantities of timber and fuel for construction of brick burning etc. [67] Huge quantities of timber were required for the purpose. The district thus must have been covered with jungle as a part of the Jungle Mahals. Even in 1869 however the jungle had largely disappeared as it appears from a paper written by the geologist Valentine Ball. [68] "The useful timber to be found in Manbhum is very limited in quantity, the forests covering but a small portion. Already the contractors and their agents have reached the hills on the Dhalbhum frontier and the rate at which sal is being cut for railway sleepers, the supply cannot last many years." [69]

Naturally the district was almost completely denuded of jungle and this inspite of the absence of Survey and Settlement operations which were held responsible in some quarters for the destruction of jungle in Ranchi and other districts. Thanks to the wasteful methods followed by the landlords and ryots, jungle practically disappeared except in the extreme north in Tundi and the foothills of Parasnath and in the extreme south on the Ayodhya range in Baghmundi and Dalma range in Barabhum. The 1918 Survey and Settlement Report showed 250 square miles of forests in Barabhum and Patkum regions, 422 square miles of forests in Sadar and 109 square miles in Dhanbad. In the Sadar, the bulk of the jungles outside parganas Barabhum and Patkum was situated in parganas Bagda and Bishpuria in Purulia thana and in the hills of Baghmundi and Jhalda. [70]

Even just a few years earlier Coupland wrote in 1910. "It is only in respect of a limited area, namely along hill ranges to the north-west of the district, that Manbhum can be described as a well-wooded country and even in these parts denudation has gone on to such an extent that the amount of large timber left, except in most inaccessible places, is very small. Small areas of protected forests are in Matha and Kailapal estates,"[71] (under protection only since 1894). Coupland's-report also brings out the fact that here and there the zamindars made special efforts to preserve small patches as shooting preserve. In ghatwali villages some sort of protection was enforced but strict application of rules in case of villages near thick population was impossible. Thus only a small percentage of ghatwali jungles were in consequence worthy of the name of forest.[72] Of the four sections therefore into which V. Ball divided the district in 1869, the first two had already disappeared as said earlier and only the last two "dry gravelly and rocky ground incapable of supporting a tree cultivation" and "land under cultivation" had proportionately increased the former owing to practice of "jhuming" or the attempt at cultivation.[73] The District Gazetteer reports that most of the forested zones of the area have degraded by biotic interference and brought about retrogression. [74]

Formerly the most deciduous forests of the district supported a wide variety of herbivores and carnivores. With the appearance of secondary forests and biotic interference, the mammal population decreased and dense luxuriant forests, elephants and tigers gradually became extinct. Smaller animals have not perished as fast as the large mammals from the district. [75] Coupland as early as 1910 reminded us to this fact by commenting that the district was singularly destitute of wild animals because of cultivation and clearing of jungles even where land is not required or suitable for cultivation. [76] Moreover hunting habits of Santals very quickly denuded the forests. He made it very clear by saying "It is possible now to travel through, and to beat miles of jungle and see not a single head of game of any description. Larger game like elephants, a stray tiger or two, rarely leopards, wolves and bear are common." [77]

If we are to summarise the entire discussion we cannot but avoid the conclusion that "woodlands" were "murdered" brutally be it by landlords, the ryots, the aboriginals and last but not the least by the Colonial Forest Policy through its hunger for valuable timber.

In 1870, about 700 square miles of jungle mahals were covered with forests though as had been seen, extensive sal forests were regularly cut which led to existence of wild coppice. The only remaining sal forests were in Midnapore jungle mahals, Zamindaris of Burdwan Division contained mostly coppice or brushwood. Some estates maintained 'rakha' jungles (kept forests) used by local villagers and useful for source of revenue to the landlord. Bankura had two thousand square miles of jungles (the decrease has been shown before by the Ishaque Report). In Nayagram and Jamboni Estates of the Midnapore jungle, Watson and company, patnidars, and the Midnapore Zamindari Company were making profits from levies on fuel wood collection. So they were deforesting the jungles by utilising the landlords' rights in wastes and jungles. In the 3,000 square miles of forests in Burdwan, very little high timber was found as firewood collection was a very lucrative profession.

Even at the end of the 19th century the state had heavily wooded areas in the western fringe of Birbhum (at Nalhati, Rajnagar, Muhammad bazar, Dubrajpur); Asansol subdivision of Burdwan, the whole of the western half of Bankura, land west of the Kasai in Midnapore and in the marshes between Kalighai and Rupnarayan in Midnapore. [78] Destruction of forests went on apace in Birbhum, Bankura and Midnapore after beginning of First World War. The need for more food production after the famine of 1943, and encouragement of the 'Grow More Food Campaign', the government fervour of which was put to unholy use by rapacious landlord and jotedar. They gave away wooded and jungly areas in settlement to hungry cultivators who delivered the coup de grace to several important private forested zones in the state.

Purulia fared no better. It is remarkable to see that only two small dots of Matha and Koilapal estates were noted to be worth conserving and in 1894 were notified as "protected forests". Though most of the other forests of this zone were surveyed and mapped the Indian Forest Act of 1865 or the later Indian Forest Act of 1878 were not applied and the Government did not take any drastic measure to stem the destruction of these private owned forests. The zamindars maintained the forests as shooting reserves, but in actual practice they engaged agents who ruthlessly destroyed the forests to earn quick profit. The tribals continued to honeycomb the luxuriant forests with patches of shifting cultivation. Land rent made a very devastating impact on the tribal community and the eco-system of their forest habitat lost its balance.

To meet the demands of Second World War recourse was taken then to certain provisions of the Indian Forest Act and negotiations with ghatwals who held certain Government Forests, started. Thus many forests of Baghmundi, Kaira, Dadhka, Ramgarh, Madhupur, Gunda came under forest management of Bihar Forest Department. At the dawn of the Forest Department, railways had triggered forest conservancy through formation of "reserves" for their fuller exploitation. Now the position was occupied by need of war. So was it "reservation" for conserving or "reservation" for exploitation? The reasons are not far to seek.

Midnapore, Bankura, Birbhum and Burdwan bore evidence of extreme erosion. In 1950-51 A. Mitra commented about forests of Burdwan "Large areas have been brought under cultivation within the last century especially in the western parts of the district which a hundred years ago were covered with Sal forests and jungles."[79]

This indiscriminate and murderous deforestation created heavy and grievous scars on the face of the country especially in the western zone where vegetation was scant. The effect has been a rude interference with the ecology of that area and rapid disappearance of wildlife on earth.

Notes & References

1. West Bengal Forests, Forest Directorate, Government of West Bengal, Centenary Commemoration volume, 1964, pp. 129-130.
2. Ibid, p. 130.
3. Ibid, p. 130.
4. Bengal District Gazetteers, Burdwan - J.C.K. Peterson, Calcutta, Bengal Secretariat Book Depot (hereafter BSBD), 1910 (BSBD).

Reprint by West Bengal District Gazetteers, Government of West Bengal, Calcutta, 1997, p. 15.

5. Ibid, p. 14.
6. Ibid, p. 14.
7. Report of the West Bengal Forest Committee, Government of Bengal, Forest and Excise Department, Superintendent, Government Printing, Bengal Government Press, Alipore, Bengal 1939, pp. 1-3.
8. Bengal District Gazetteers - Bankura by L.S.S. O'Malley, Calcutta, BSBD; 1908, Reprint by West Bengal, Calcutta, 1995, p. 9.
9. Ibid, p. 13.
10. Ibid, p. 13.
11. Ibid, pp. 12-13.
12. Ibid, pp. 14-15.
13. Ibid, p. 16.
14. F.W. Robertson - Final Report on the Survey and Settlement Operation in the District of Bankura 1917 - 1924. (Calcutta, Bengal Secretariat Book Depot, 1926).
15. H.S.M. Ishaque, OBE, I.C.S. Superintendent, Government Printing, West Bengal Government Press, Alipore, West Bengal, 11th August, 1947, p. 36, Government of Bengal, Department of Agriculture, Forests and Fisheries, Agricultural Statistics by Plot to Plot Enumeration in Bengal, 1944 and 1945, Part II.
16. Ibid, p. 36.
17. Ranjan Kumar Gupta, *The Economic life of a Bengal District Birbhum 1770--1857*, University of Burdwan, 1984, p. 2.
18. L.S.S. O'Malley, Bengal District Gazetteers, Birbhum, Calcutta, The Bengal Secretariat Book Depot (BSBD) 1910, Reprint by West Bengal District Gazetteers, Govemment of West Bengal, Calcutta, 1996. p. 7.
19. Ranjan Kumar Gupta, op.cit., p. 10.
20. L.S.S. O'Malley, Birbhum, op.cit., p. 6.
21. J.E. Gastrell, *Report on the District of Bankura (1863)*, p. 5.
22. L.S.S. O'Malley, Birbhum, op.cit., p. 57.
23. Ibid, pp. 79-80.
24. Ibid, p. 6.
25. W. S. Sherwill, *Geographical and Statistical Report of the District of Beerbhoom*, Calcutta, 1855, p. 31, cited in Edward Duyker, *Tribal*

Guerrillas : The Santals of West Bengal and the Naxalite Movement, Delhi, 1987, p. 146.

26. C. Keating to Board of Revenue, 30th August, 1789.
27. Collector of Rajshahi to Collector of Birbhum, 26th December, 1788.
28. *Bengal District Gazetteers, Birbhum*, L.S.S. O'Malley, Calcutta, The Bengal Secretariat Book Depot, 1910, Reprint by West Bengal District Gazetteers, Government of West Bengal, Calcutta, 1996. pp. 6-7.
29. W.W. Hunter, *The Annals of Rural Bengal*, London, Smith Elder and Company 1868, Reprint by West Bengal District Gazetteers, Government of West Bengal, Calcutta, 1999, p. 60.
30. Ibid, p. 147.
31. Bengal District Gazetteers, Birbhum, L.S.S. O'Malley, Bengal District Gazetteers, Birbhum, op.cit., pp. 6-7.
32. Ibid, p. 7.
33. Final Report on the Survey and Settlement of the Santhali Villages of Rampurhat and several other villages in the Rampurhat and Sub divisions of the District of Birbhum, 1904-1914 By P.M. Robertson, Settlement Officer, Calcutta, Bengal Secretariat Book Depot, 1915, p. 7.
34. Forest Committee, 1939, op.cit., pp. 1-3.
35. Ishaque Report, op.cit.
36. Bengal District Gazetteers, Midnapore, By L.S.S. O'Malley, Calcutta, The Bengal Secretariat Book Depot, 1911, Reprint by West Bengal District Gazetteers, Government of West Bengal, Calcutta, 1995, p. 15.
37. Ibid, p. 16.
38. West Bengal Forests, Forest Directorate, Government of West Bengal, Centenary Commemoration Volume, 1964, p. 149.
39. O'Malley, Midnapore, op.cit., p. 16.
40. Ibid, O'Malley, p. 16.
41. Ibid, p. 16.
42. A.K. Jameson - Final Report on the Survey and Settlement operations in the District of Midnapore, 1911-1917 (Calcutta, B.S.B.D, 1918)
43. Report of the West Bengal Forest Committee, op.cit. pp. 1-3.
44. Ishaque Report, op.cit.

45. O'Malley, Midnapore, op.cit., p. 17.
46. Gazetteer of India, West Bengal, Purulia, West Bengal District Gazetteers. Purulia, 1985, Government of West Bengal, Chapter I, p. 1.
47. D.C. Sircar, *Cosmography and Geography in Early Indian Literature, in Indian Studies; Past and Present*, Vol. VII, No. 3, Calcutta, 1996, p. 260.
48. Surajit Sinha, *Ethnic groups, villages and town of pargana, Barabhum*, Calcutta 1964, p. 7.
49. L.S.S. O'Malley, Bengal District Gazetteers, Bankura, op.cit.
50. Ibid, p. 45.
51. Purulia - West Bengal District Gazetteer, op.cit., p. 7.
52. Valentine Ball, *Notes on the Flora of Manbhum; Joumal of Asiatic Society of Bengal* (JASB) 38 (e) : pp. 112-25, 1869.
53. Bengal District Gazetteers, Manbhum, H. Coupland, op.cit.
54. Ibid, pp. 10 -11
55. Ibid, p. 11.
56. Ibid, p. 11.
57. G.S. Puri, *Indian Forest Ecology*, Vol. 1, New Delhi, 1960, pp. 89-90.
58. Report on the Forest Administration in the Chotonagpore Division of Bengal, By W. Schlich, Inspector General of Forests to the Government of India, dated 14th February, 1885, Calcutta, Printed by the Superintendent of Government of India Press, 1885, pp. 1-2.
59. Ibid, p. 2.
60. Ibid, p. 5.
61. Ibid, p. 5.
62. Working Plan for the Reserved and Protected and Private Protected Forests of Manbhum Division (As it existed prior to November 1956). Prepared by J.N. Sinha, Conservator of Forests, Development Circle Under Direction of Chief Conservator of Forests, Bihar, Printed by the Superintendent, Secretariate Press, Bihar, Patna, 1962, pp. 25-30.
63. Final Report of the Survey and Settlement operations in the District of Manbhum, 1918-1925, By B.K. Gokhale, I.C.S. Settlement Officer, Chotanagpore, Patna, Superintendent, Government Printing press, Bihar and Orissa, 1928, p. 69.

64. Ibid, p. 69.
65. Ibid, p. 70.
66. Ibid, p. 68.
67. Report on Forest Administration by W. Schlich, op.cit., p. 7.
68. V. Ball, op.cit., pp. 112-125.
69. ibid, p. 122.
70. Settlement Report, Manbhum, op.cit., p. 68.
71. H. Coupland, Bengal Districts Gazetteers, Manbhum, op.cit., p. 11.
72. Ibid, p. 11.
73. Coupland, op.cit., p. 11.
74. West Bengal District Gazetteer, Purulia, op.cit., p. 45.
75. Ibid, p. 59.
76. Coupland, op.cit., p. 21.
77. Coupland, op.cit., p. 21.
78. Census-1951 West Bengal, Land and Land Revenue Department, A. Mitra, An account of land management in West Bengal, 1870-1950.

5

Man and the Beast : Changing Perspectives from Punthi to Prose

Sutapa Chatterjee-Sarkar

The present paper attempts to analyse two distinct but inter-connected genres of representation – the punthi and the prose – that emerged in the context of the Sundarbans, its historical experience and development. While neither of these genres can be said to constitute a self-conscious discursive aiming at autonomous management of community resources or of the region in the centuries of colonization.

This paper is an attempt to compare these two genres of literature associated with the Sundarbans and to draw certain general conclusions about the nature of material change in the environment between the 18th and the 20th centuries, about community's attitudes to environment, and the mental world of the Bengali middle class that sought to reconstruct a new idea of the Sundarbans in their literary exercise. Punthi literature is concerned with the emergence of popular cults, which reflects the immediate concerns of the community. Concerns are very directly environmental battling against a hostile environment. The tiger is a metaphor for the harsh material pressure of the situation.

Punthi Literature

Between the seventeenth and nineteenth centuries there thrived in lower deltaic Bengal a *punthi* literature in Bengali verse devoted to the god and goddesses of the Sundarbans. This literature reflected a mental outlook specific to the natural terrain that gave birth to it. Its theme was the struggle between humanity and nature. This literature catered to and arose from the mental requirements of the lowest and the most marginal elements of the population. Their beliefs stood apart from the mainstream Hinduism and Islam of the higher classes. Folk religion here, as represented by local syncretic cults, had a distinctive aura of its own. They were the god and goddesses of woodcutters, honey gatherers, beeswax gatherers, boat builders, and the most desperate cultivators.

The Sundarban literature sprang up before the British became fully hegemonic in Bengal, so that it may not be very practical to expect it to be affected in its essential features by the colonial context. In this sense this is a particular form of the literature of transition in the late pre-colonial and early colonial Bengal. This gives us a view of the mental world and life conditions of the people, which is not accessible from other historical sources of the period. The life and condition of the habitants of the Sundarbans are explained here as they were before the advent of British power in Bengal.

It needs to be noted that settlements in the Sundarbans go back to a long antiquity. Recent archaeological findings have proved beyond doubt that ports and settlements had sprung up and disappeared recurrently in deltaic Bengal in the last two thousand years. Clearings would spring up from time to time, only to be overtaken by some natural or political calamity.

It is necessary at this stage to recount the possibilities of livelihood in this inhospitable terrain. It is these sources of danger that formed the underlying theme of the Sundarban *Punthi* literature. The people of the area had not been equipped with firearms to any appreciable extent as late as the end of the nineteenth century. The ground was too swampy to explore on foot. The only roots of the communication were the waterways. The land was notorious for its wildlife: tigers, snakes, crocodiles, etc.

The life of the people was always at the mercy of these creatures. Every time a sizeable portion of people developed a regular habitation, the settlement faced constant cyclone hazards floods and other natural calamities. Jungle animals starved of forest foods, ventured into the inhabited villages in search of prey. The Royal Bengal Tiger of Sundarbans was said to be a habitual man-eater, unlike other tigers. One of the central motifs of the *punthis* under consideration was man's struggle against wild animals, especially the tiger, idealized into a monstrous foe, and sometimes a subordinate deity.

The population of Sundarban consisted entirely of marginalized people. 'Nearly all the inhabitants' of the Sundarbans were 'either Hindus or Muslims' according to Hunter. 'There were of course, a few *Magh* Buddhists: and native Christians also came up with missionary penetration of Portuguese and later British power. The rest belonged to the Hindu and Muslim communities, most of low status.'

The native Christians, as recorded by Hunter, were all cultivators. There were also other tribes like Santals, Mundas, and Oraons who had come and settled in this area for reclaiming the forest. All these people depended entirely on the natural economy of the forest for their livelihood and they had to struggle perpetually against the natural hazards. As their weapons were woefully inadequate, the people came to bank mentally on divine intervention. A superstitious fatalism pervaded the folk cults. The following is a discussion of a few texts originating from this conjecture and reflecting the woes of the people.

The text dealt with here is the *Raimangal.* It eulogizes the tiger god Dakshin Ray and was written in the year 1686 by Krisna Ram Das. Later it was edited and published by Satyanarayan

Bhattyacharya on behalf of the Calcutta University. There is also an incomplete undated manuscript of the *Raimangal* by Rudradev. This was published in the Sahitya Prakasika, Vol. V, Dwadash Mangal, ed. Panchanan Mondal, Santiniketan, 1966.

These texts are all written in simple verse. It is well known that the people chanted some verses before they entered the forest so that no danger would befall them. What necessitated the appearance of these texts? Why did they disseminate among so many people over so long a span of time? If construction of a text is understood as a social function, what kind of investment (aesthetic, or moral, or religious, or political) valorized these texts? What purpose did they serve that a body of people could use them in the course of their daily lives? At first glance, these texts would appear to be fantastic narratives about gods, goddesses and their interactions with humble men and women. Taken as documents of social reality, such texts would be poor in factual content.

But these texts were meant not to depict reality, but to transform it magically. After all, they were meant to be read as 'mantras', to be chanted during the propitiatory rites. This function is not unique to these texts alone. There is a genre in Bengali literature, the origin of which is lost in obscurity, called the *Mangal Kabya*; later there was the *panchali*. These texts belong to this *Mangal Kabya – panchali* tradition.

The formal rhetorical character of these (the rhythm, the metre and all other literary devices of narration) bears ample testimony to what we have said just now. Panchali is written in an easy flowing verse meant to facilitate the act of reciting. It describes the acts of grace of a god or a goddess and is to be read out during or after the act of worship of that deity's image or idol. The worship and the recitation is meant to transform reality magically, rendering it favourable for the devotee. Thus there are: the panchali of Lakshmi (the goddess of riches);of Sitala (small pox goddess); of Manasha (snake goddess); and of late, thanks to the movies, of Santoshi Ma. Worship of a particular god or goddess by recitation of his or her panchali is meant to ward off a particular kind of evil. Consequently, these texts at hand are replete with verses where promises are made by the god or goddess to confer a particular favour or ward off a particular danger. It is these that are desired by the devotee and attributed to the deity.

Let us turn now to the narratives of the text.

DAKSHIN RAY

Dakshin Ray, known as the supreme lord of tigers, is widely worshipped throughout the whole of the Sundarban in both parts of Bengal even today. He is usually sitted upon a tiger and is often accompanied by his brother or companion Kalu Ray. Dakshin Ray is worshipped not only as the god of tigers but also as a divine curer. From one of the stories we come to know that he is the son of Shiva. The head of Ganesa when severed from his body fell in the south to become a deity. This is perhaps how the name Dakshin Ray came into being – as a subordinate alternative to the idea of Ganesa or Ganapati.

From the legend of *Raimangal* written by Krishna Ram Das, we get the following story. Pushpa Datta, a merchant of Bardaha, intended to brave the dangers at sea in search of his lost father. He asked Ratai Baulya to supply the wood for his boats.

Dinga gathaiba sadhu patane jaite
adesh karilo karya katiya anite
chalila shiropa paiya baulya ratai
loia pradhan putra ar chhoy bhai

....

....

Katite lagila kastha monomoto jata
kiropa pusuri sundri adi kato.

With the intention to set sail Pushpa Datta asked Baulya Ratai to fell trees for wood. Ratai along with his elder son and six brothers went to fetch the wood. They selected trees in the forest according to their liking – Kiropa, Pusuri, Sundari and began to fell them. As they were about to return, they came across a large tree.

Dakshin rayer ek briksha puja mani
seito bonete ache keho nahi jani
dekhiya dagar gachh sobe meli kate
tilek bilamba kara paramad ghate
dakshin rayer krodh ihato janiya
adeshila chhoy bagh nikate aniya
mamuda kumuda suda bagh tangabhanga
bajradanta khan daura chakshu jar ranga
samukhe rahila tara kariya pranam
hailo rayer rayer aagya bale krishnaram.

There was a tree in the wood, which was the abode of Dakshin Ray. Not knowing what it was, they began to fell it as it appeared to be so large. Calamity occurred soon as there appeared six angry tigers with bloodshot eyes, Mamuda, Kumuda, Suda, Tangabhanga, Bajradanta and Khan Daura. Bowing before Dakshin Ray, they stood before him. The Ray, says Krishnaram, issued orders.

The tigers pounced on Ratai's brothers and killed them all. He was about to commit suicide when a heavenly voice asked him to sacrifice his son to Dakshin Ray in order to resurrect his brothers. Ratai obeyed the advice and his six brothers were revived. His son too regained his life. Ratais and his brothers returned and narrated the supernatural powers of Dakshin Ray to the local people.

Pushpa Datta then offered a bag of gold coins to the craftsmen who would make the boats for him. At the command of Mahadeva, the master of heaven, two craftsmen, Hanuman and Biswakarma, descended to the earth in the form of human beings and made seven boats in the next seven days. The best boat was named the *Madhukar.*

Pushpa Datta resolved to set out on an arduous journey across the sea in search of his missing father. Sushila, Pushpa Datta's mother, offered prayers to Dakshin Ray and entreated him to save her son from any danger. She advised Pushpa:

Jakhan bipak dekho samshay jivan
Bhabio dakshin rai charan

Whenever you are in trouble or life is at stake seek shelter at the feet of Dakshin Ray.

Pushpa Datta began his journey aboard the Madhukar. On the way he worshipped Siva at Barasat and reached Khania where he offered prayers to Dakshin Ray. There he came across an alter of Ghazi Sahab. On enquiry, the boatman explained that in the past there had been a confrontation between Dakshin Ray and Ghazi Sahab. Neither of them could win. The fighting was fierce. Various tigers took part in the battle. The first disciple and most favourite tiger of Ghazi Sahab was 'Dauda' and that of Dakshin Ray was 'Hira'.

Prathame ailo bagh nam rupchanda
samukher danta tar sona diya bandha
mariya boner hati jar ghar bhaksha
rakshas palai dare kiba dana daksha
kashuya bagher mashua baes kalo sara
duta chakshu jale jano akasher tara

First appeared the tiger Rupchanda whose fore teeth were enameled with gold. He killed wild elephants and ate them at home and even the demons were afraid of him. Next came the tiger Kashuya whose eyes were burning bright like stars. Realizing that the prolonged fight meant destruction of the whole earth, God appeared in the garb of a saint and mediated between them. In accordance with the agreement, Dakshin Ray was to be the master of the Southern district and the Ghazi Sahab the master of the Hijli region. It was also agreed that every devotee would pay equal respect to Dakshin Ray and Ghazi Sahab.

Moving down the lower reaches of Ganga, Pushpa Datta arrived at its confluence with the sea at Ganga Sagar. There he heard the story of how Bhagirath had brought the Ganga down to the earth. He sailed along the coasts and at Rajdaha came across a wonderful sight – a beautiful place on the sea. His companions, however, could not see it. Finally Pushpa Datta arrived at Turanga where he narrated to the king his experience of the wonderful sight. The king, who was not inclined to believe the fanciful story, asked him for proof. Pushpa Datta could not show him the wonderful sight. He was imprisoned and king ordered that he should be beheaded.

Pushpa Datta prayed to Dakshin Ray for help. Next day when he was about to be executed Dakshin Ray appeared there. An army of tigers accompanied him. The tigers attacked the city and the king lost his life. A heavenly voice at the battlefield promised the queen that her husband would be revived; but she must worship Dakshin Ray and give her daughter in marriage to Pushpa Datta. The queen agreed, and the king and his soldiers regained their lives. The merchant's father who had been imprisoned by the king was released. Pushpa Datta married the princess Ratnabati, and along with his father and newly wed wife, returned to his country. The fame of Dakshin Ray spread far and wide.

Tabe narapatibar kayabakyamane
pujila rayer pad bibidha bidhane
ghare ghare jato lok pujila sakal
dakshin rayer mane baro kutuhal
pitaputra duijane harashita mon
pujila rayer pad parama jatan

Then the king offered prayers from his heart to Dakshin Ray, worshipping him in accordance with the laid down rituals. In every house, men began to worship him. This stirred Dakshin Ray deeply. Father and son joined in joyous prayer at his feet.

In addition to Krishnaram Das's *Raimangal* there is also an incomplete manuscript of *Raimangal* by Rudradev. This is notable on account of the depiction of the highly individualized traits of several tigers. In fact each tiger has a well-defined personality in Rudradev's version. 'Huma Mahateja', for example, the king of tigers who headed the eighty-four tigers summoned by Dakshin

Ray in the war against Barakhan Ghazi, gave the following account of himself to Dakshin Ray.

Kendabane kaidaro sarir dagar baro
chalite na pari ati bara
nahi kore chalbul pare thake khaler kula
keora boner madhye ara
dari pai sari gai suye thake khai dai
hanoi samai ami asi
nidre jai neye naker nises peye
kachi dhore tani bose bose
nouka lagayai bhite lap diye pari tate
ghare dhori loi ek jan.

I am the tough one of the Kenda woods. My body is extremely big. I cannot move fast. I do not move about. I crouch in the Keora woods by the side of the creek, waiting for the oarsmen who row down singing the sari song. As they lie down after taking their meals, I come out. The boatmen are asleep and I can hear them breathe through their nostrils [sic]. I am in no hurry as I sit down. Calmly I pull the rope and bring the boat slowly to the mud bank. I jump down upon the boat and seize one of them by the neck.

Rudradev gives the description of the tigers' attack on the fakirs.

Gaganer tara jeno nayan ghurai
lap diye pare bagh phakirer gai
ghar bhenge rakta khai chhire phele mundu
kamre phakir that kare khanda khanda.

The tiger's eyes shone like the stars of the sky. It jumped upon the fakir, and drank the blood from his neck after ripping apart his head. It tore the fakir's body to pieces with its teeth.

The world of the folk deities delineated above offers important insights into the character of Past human settlements in the Sundarbans. It tells us that in all probability the land had been sparsely populated. Prosperous cities, as Satish Mitra and Kalidas Datta would have us believe, imply social relations and religious beliefs of a higher order. But in the folk tales of the Sundarbans, the prevalence of tiger gods and goddesses point to a more primordial context. Settlements such as Chandraketugarh were nothing more than trade outposts and were too unstable to survive.

The folk gods of the Sundarbans are depicted in the narrative as arbitrary deities, exercising a fearful command over the settlers. The reasons are presumably twofold. First, the deities emerged out of the hard material struggle for existence in an inhospitable terrain. They had to invent the heavenly deities in order to come to terms with the overwhelming forces of nature. The god and goddesses were personifications of the malignant forces that had to be propitiated. If the ritual propitiation was done properly, then it was calculated that a living could be made out of the forest. And therefore no moral virtue was attached to the gods and goddesses. Secondly, the settlers were all of lowly origin, and the deities were destined to dominate a lesser breed. Therefore, the narrators invest in them all the attributes of the arbitrary master.

The most striking common feature of these tales is a reward-punishment syndrome. Not infrequently the deities are shown by their narrators to be engaged in fierce battles, and the deity who eventually won the duel, drew the largest number of followers. Sometimes, when a potential devotee was adversely disposed to the deity, and declined to deify the latter as an idol of veneration at his homestead, the deity descended upon him, inflicted a crushing punishment, and compelled him to be a faithful follower instead of a recalcitrant opponent.

Internecine bickerings gripped the community of people and even their god-lings. In each and every local tale we invariably notice close encounters between the two communities – the Hindus and the Muslims, and in the process of confrontation communal harmony was established in the end. This is the natural inference to be drawn from the tales of the deities. The god and goddesses waged war with one another over the supremacy of the jungle. In the sequel, they either came to an amicable division of rule and understanding among themselves, or a god of a higher order descended from the heavenly abode and mediated the quarrel.

The inference from both the cases is however the same. It was, one can argue, a question of survival. The adage 'survival of the fittest ' was, however, not accepted as a norm here. The people, nay the gods, learnt through experience the wise principle of adjustment and accommodation. The people adjusted to the existence of religious divisions, sometimes voluntarily, but more often under duress. This accommodative principle permeated their religious practices too. A struggling population, with whom the question of survival was of the utmost importance, sought to accommodate one another and to propitiate every god or goddesses who held sway in the jungle.

Representing the Environment in the Prose Literature

The Bengali prose literature of the twentieth century gave a new meaning to the idea of Sundarban in Bengali consciousness. In contrast to the earlier *Punthi* literature which had reflected elements of popular local mentality, the new stories were expressions of an emerging middle class viewpoint.

The new prose literature was in the nature of a direct social narrative of the life of the region. Here stories had a definite structure, form and social message. Most of the stories depict the life of the settlers in the Sundarbans while continuing to draw on the old and intimate relationship between man and nature. Nature even shaped the life cycle of the people and their religion, human bondage based on love and finally it explained the social dependence on jungle for livelihood. Yet at the end there was a sad tone in these stories lamenting the steady disappearance of the jungle, which sustained human life in the region. In the new prose form nature becomes a differentiated category as against that in the old form (*punthi*) where nature was part and parcel of the undifferentiated mythical and existential whole.

Settlers in the Sundarbans throughout the period had to brave salinity, frequent floods and occasional cyclones to make cultivation possible there. The annual harvest, notwithstanding their untiring efforts, was insufficient to feed all the mouths round the year. Evidently, they had to depend for subsistence on forest products to make up for the deficit. Collecting honey, wax, wood, golpatta, etc. became part of their routine duties. Thus the forest became an inseparable part of their lives.

After the land reclamation had started, noted the literature, during the British rule improvement of transport facilities took place and new settlers came and settled in this region. This brought about a definite break in the social composition there. Among them were agents of zamindars, forest officers who patrolled the forests and the rivers and bheri managers. Another group of people came in search of living, having been edged out by the competitive atmosphere of commercially more developed areas. There were also fugitives from towns and cities who had run away to escape from the regulated strictures of moral conduct of more organized societies.

With increasing urban intrusion there evolved an interestingly new social structure that was quite different from the one previously existing in this region. This was reflecting in a number of stories written in the twentieth century romanticizing the Sundarbans. Written in Bengali prose these stories depict the changing mentality of these settlers as a whole, who were now aggressively reclaiming wastelands and adventuring into the woods, protected with fire-arms at times, for the sheer fun of hunting in the wilderness.

Other than the settlers from north, the *Magh* who formed a part of the population still remained in this area. Bibhuti Bandopadhyay in his *Sundarbane Satbachhar* and Narayan Gangopadhyay's *Upanibesh* gives a description of the life of *Magh* pirates in this area.

The changing social order brought about a revolution in the attributes of the settlers considered as a single community and a conflict of mentalities grew between the earlier and latter ones, between wastelands (Bada) and habitation (Abade). The prose literature captured this mood in quite effective contrast to the mentality depicted in the *punthis*. While the original settlers had an unrestricted access to the jungle, now, they were afraid of being detected by forest officers on patrol (Pitel Babus). The change was very rapid and it has been clearly depicted in the stories.

In the *punthis*, religion had been the dominant element, so much so that the tigers were looked upon with fearful respect as sons of Banbibi, the deity of the forest. As a consequence, the settlers had never tried to kill tigers unless tigers attacked them. Similar attitudes applied to snakes, who were likewise related to Goddesses Masasha. In the story 'Arjun Sardar' by Shib Shankar Mitra, it is seen how Fatima, Arjan's wife, is always against her husband's going out on a hunt. Shib Shankar Mitra in his Royal Bengaler Atmakatha gives a clear depiction of the life of a tiger in this region. This could not be thought of earlier on. Two aspects are noteworthy – that it was an autobiography of a tiger and their waning importance as Banbibi's sons.

The prose literature, different enough, depicts them as games to the newly settled urban middle class, thus showing how religion had at least partially wanted in dominance. However, its powers could not be totally disregarded as some old customs were still practised and a few beliefs still prevailed. The new setters also came under their influence.

A very interesting story would be that of the Baulés or Fakirs. They were archetypal chasers of tigers who lived in austerity like a separate socio-religious class. Baulés were not able to marry for few years as a consequence of the penance they had pledged to undergo. Each Baulé was to look after the particular chak as the ancient chieftain and as a religious custom could not turn his back on anyone who called for help.

The middle class in spite of being well equipped with fire-arms, could not gather enough courage to invade the jungle without a Baulé evidently more out of fear originating from superstition rather than anything else. Apart from acting as tiger-chasers, they also acted as local healers. The widespread dependence on Baulés was thus a remarkable feature of the Sundarbans.

Fakirs who gave medicine still formed a dominant class in this area. People took usual medicines (Homeopathy etc.) and at the same time went to Fakirs for treatment. The middle class could not totally deny the power of Fakirs and Baulés. They were, in fact, quite afraid of them.

The most important departure from the previously prevailing mentality of the settlers was perhaps the sense of bravado and the expectation of reward in connection with hunting. Firearms became the dominant mode of communication between jungle and man. The earlier fear of unknown was replaced by a desire to conquer. Guns thus revolutionized the relationship between man and jungle. The stories often written from middle class prism romanticized and mystified the new spirit of fighting. Fear was replaced by a spirit of adventure. This new phenomenon evidently had not been reflected in the earlier form of *punthi* literature.

As habitation encroached and the jungle receded, contradictions emerged. In Shib Shankar Mitra's 'Arjan Sardar' we find that Arjan at one point was asked to kill a pregnant dear. This according to old religious order, would have been considered a heinous crime. Arjan did not want to shoot. But he was forced to do that by the new comers in the jungle (like Rashid Babu) who would otherwise throw him out of job. As the latter settlers gradually became the dominant class, they established their own rules which were designed to cater to their class interest. Deforestation progressed at an unprecedented rate and the original settlers were exploited fuming discontent and tension mounted in this region. This culminated into peasant uprising (Tebhaga struggle) of 1946.

These stories give us a detailed picture of newly grown middle class settlements where earlier only low class people inhabited. But this gave the region a heterogeneous character. Middle class, whose direct participation in the venture was negligible, romanticized the tales of Sundarban, the hunting spirit of the local people, perhaps, to fill up the gap of lack of participation in the real adventure. The receding of the jungle made the middle class more romantic about it.

Earlier stories like *Byghra* and *Damaru Charit* were fantasies and give the readers an idea of the region that was untrue. These stories and anecdotes were supposed to have the elements of sparkling falsities that would portray a picture away from reality. The region being unknown to most of the people made it easier for the writers to circulate any absurd fantasy about the area. However, the ones written later on were true depictions of life in the Sundarbans. Stories of Mahesh and Arjan actually portray how life was – full of struggle for survival – in this region. The narrative of the various stories will help to understand the situation.

The narratives dealt with here are:

1. 'Mahesh Sardar' in Bane Jangale by Jogendranath Sarkar, Calcutta, 1929, reprint edition by Naba Prakash, Calcutta, 1989.
2. 'Bhu' by Shankar Basu in Badar Galpa, Calcutta, 1977.
3. 'Royal Bengaler Atmakatha' by Shib Shankar Mitra, Calcutta, 1983, Reprint edition 'Sundarban Samagra', Ananda Publishers, Calcutta, 1988.

MAHESH SARDAR

Stories of the famous hunters of the Sundarbans remain incomplete unless we know about the stories of Mahesh Sardar written by Jogindranath Sarkar.

One of the stories goes as follows – Mahesh was on his way back home from the zamindar's 'cutchery'. It was already dark and he carried only a heavy stick suitable for fighting with fierce animals to defend himself against any plausible attacks. Since he was getting late, he took a short cut through the jungle to his house. When he had almost reached home, a tiger attacked him. While the tiger jumped over a creek, Mahesh, showing great courage and ready intelligence, pushed the stick into its mouth and down the throat with all his might. As he firmly held the other end against his legs, the tiger, now in great pain, was apparently immobilized. Hearing its moan, Mahesh's younger brother came to the spot to his rescue and they then together killed the tiger.

In another account, a tiger was found to be frequently attacking a village. When a pregnant woman was carried away one day, the villagers lost patience and went out in the jungle in a team under Mahesh Sardar's leadership to intercept it and then kill it. Near the spot where they discovered the remains of the woman's body, a man was suddenly pounced upon from the back. Though he was strong and fought valiantly he received severe injuries. Mahesh, decided not to shoot lest it killed the man, picked up an axe and thrust deadly blows on the tigers back. As the animal lunged at him, he dodged away to a distance and thereafter again hacked the animal till death by almost chopping its head off its shoulder.

These tales not only glorify the courage and physical strength of one man, they also give us a lively record of the dangers that enmeshed into the day-to-day lives of the people of the region. There is a sensation of bravado in connection with the glory of hunting as well as consequential to the prospect of receiving rewards. A spirit of adventure replaced fear. This was absent in the *punthi* literature.

BHU

Another story written by Shankar Basu in his *Badar Galpa* gives a clear picture of the peasant discontent and deplorable situation of landless labourers in this region. The story begins with an appeal for ownership registration of land and compensation charges for harassment by Smt. Jaynab Bibi. The story unfolds to reveal that Fazlar, Jaynab's husband, had given her a small plot of land after their marriage. This plot of land was a part of the jungle of Sundarban which was cleared and made arable by Kachi Rahman, Fazlar's grandfather. Kachi Rehman was an easy-going and cool-tempered person, who finally lost his temper when the local zamindar took away all his land and even robbed him of his adolescent daughter. Kachi Rehman then killed the zamindar and ran away to the Sundarbans.

Fazlar and Jaynab spent their time labouring for that one plot of land all day, but finally lost it to Kamana Pal, the local money-lender through interests for a small sum of money they had loaned from him for buying seeds. The appeal was against that. But of course, the only order that was issued by the court was an injunction in favour of Kamana Pal.

Then followed a period of utter poverty and deprivation for Fazlar and Jaynab with their small son. Around this time, the long-suppressed anger of the peasants finally erupted in the form of the Tebhaga Movement. Fazlar obviously joined it. This part of the story ends with Jaynab seeing Fazlar being killed by the police shooting at him.

The second part of the story deals with Abu Hassim Rahman, the only son of Fazlar who managed to survive the terrible days of poverty after his father's death. We also see him lodging a case against Hamid Laskar, to whom Kamana Pal sold the plot of land he had usurped from Fazlar. It is revealed that Abu was a bargadar under Hamid Laskar, but there was no legally valid documentation of the fact. Now Hamid was ousting Abu being a defaulter in paying up debts. Abu went to court as a last resort, hoping that through the Land Reforms Act of 1956, he would be able to get back the plot of land that really was his by inheritance, the plot of land which his great grandfather had made arable through his own labour and for which his father had died.

The story ends on the extremely sad note of another injunction in favour of Hamid Laskar being declared and Abu realizing that his father's rebellion and death changed nothing for the poor peasants.

Royal Bengaler Atmakatha

Shib Shankar Mitra has played a dual role. At one hand he has written stories which show how the scenario changed with the reclamation of the jungle and on the other hand he has also given a detailed account of the life of the Royal Bengal Tiger in the Sundarbans. Twentieth century prose literature is very different from the *punthis*. The tigers in the prose literature are treated as animals only, they are no longer sons of gods. They are the main attraction of the hunters. They were attacked for the sheer fun of hunting which was never imagined during the days of the *punthi* literature. Mitra in his narrative *Royal Bengaler Atmakatha* writes about the tiger in the bada (jungle) region. Their life and their attitude towards the human beings. Here even the relationship between the tiger and the crocodile is also dealt with. Those two are the ruling beasts of the jungle. This narrative also throws light on the behaviour of the tigers with the human beings.

The writers claim that this is an account, written in human language of course, of what a Royal Bengal Tiger of the Sundarbans would say if he could communicate to us in our idiom. This account is supposed to be based on the author's understanding of the behaviour and characteristics of Royal Bengal Tigers, gained both through his own wanderings in the Sundarbans as well as from the various tales he had heard from the settlers of the region.

In this account, the author describes how a tiger grows up in the forest, how fiercely the mother tigress guards her young while he is small, how she trains him up to be a predator himself and how she finally leaves him alone once he is fit to survive on his own. This narrative further describes how tigers distinguish between different areas of the forest and what are the different techniques they use to hunt different animals. It is stressed here that, tigers never hunt unless they are hungry.

According to this account, these two ruling beasts of this region, crocodile and tiger, treat each other with mutual respect and normally avoid encounters between themselves. However, in case of a fight between the two, there is no predicting the winner – for they are both equally powerful and cunning. In fact, it often results in both being killed.

Mitra's narrative describes how a tiger comes to sexual maturity, how they choose their own mates and what exactly is the relationship between a tiger and a tigress during the mating season. It is maintained that, a tiger or a tigress never cohabits with more than one partner in one mating season. It is also stated that, once the tigress has conceived, her sexual urges reduce – which often cause problems between the partners if conception occurs too early in the mating season. The cohabitation breaks down once the tigress has delivered the cubs; because, tigers are jealous of the cubs while tigresses are fierce in their affection.

A large portion of this narrative deals with the relationship between the Royal Bengal Tiger and the people of the Sundarbans who often have to tread the jungles for various attempts at collecting different means of subsistence from the forest. It is stressed that the Sundarban tigers are as wary of human beings as the latter are wary of tigers. From sons of Banbibi, they thus become subjects of sport.

Conclusion

As the habitation encroached and the jungle receded, changes became prominent. With the gradual penetration of colonial administration into the land relationship, the agrarian system evolved into an egalitarian land structure. The virgin land attracted the low caste peasant cultivators, who reclaimed land from ever expanding jungle. These people faced all the difficulties and even fought with the dangers of death. But the expanding population and production of surplus led to the emergence of land holding community who had their share in the land revenue. These initiated a politics of conflict between the peasant cultivators and agrarian landlords. Soon discontent and tension culminated into agitation (Tebhaga Movement of 1946).

Thus, we see that the *punthis* and the later novels constituted the images of two different worlds – one of a rural intimate, communitarian life, mystic and myth being its primary signifiers and the other of an urban differentiated, hierarchised life ridden by secular strife and ruthless exploitation. Although both the representations focused on the theme of struggle; yet it was conceived differently, both in terms of contestants and its overall implication. Banbibi and Dakshin Ray having left the battlefield, it was now a struggle of man against man.

Notes and References

1. Gopendra Krishna Basu, Banglar Loukik Deb Debi, 1966, pp. 10 –11.
2. Ibid, p. 43.
3. Abdul Jalil, Sundarbaner Itihaas, 2nd edition, Dacca, 1986, pp. 418 – 420.
4. W.W Hunter, A Statistical Account of Bengal, Vol.1, District of the Twenty four Parganas and the Sundarbans, Reprint edition, Delhi, 1973, pp. 317 – 318.
5. Ibid.
6. Manindranath Jana, Sundarbaner Samaj O Sanskriti, Calcutta, 1984, pp. 100 – 101.
7. Gopendra Krishna Basu, Op. cit, p. 9.
8. Sarat Chandra Mitra, On an Accumulation Drole from Eastern Bengal and on a Musalmani Legend about the Sylvan Saint Banbibi and their deity Dakshin Ray, Calcutta, 1923, pp 154 – 55; Gopendra Krishna Basu, op. cit, p.154.
9. Ibid, p.146.
10. Satyanarayan Bhattacharya (ed.) Raimangal, Sahitya Sabha, Bardhaman, 1956 (1363), p.5.
11. Ibid, p.89.
12. Rudradev, Raimangal, (incomplete manuscript),Panchnan Mandal (ed.) Sahitya Prakasika Vol.V., Dwadash Mangal, Santiniketan, 1966, p.128.
13. Purnendu Ghosh, Tebhagar Smriti, Madhya Pradesh, 1987, pp. 6 – 7; Tapan Bhattacharya, Rahasyamayi Sundarban, Vol.1, Calcutta, 1988, p.3; Shib Shankar Mitra, Bede Baule in Sundarban Samagra, Calcutta, 1988, pp. 16 – 17.

14. West Bengal State Archives, Revenue Department, Land Revenue Branch, File no. 11-R-45g 1931, Proceedings no. 1- 4, March 1932, Report on the Land Revenue Administration of the Presidency of Bengal for the year 1931 – 32; W.W. Hunter, Vol.1, op. cit, p. 319 – 320.
15. Shib Shankar Mitra, Sundarban in Sundarban Samagra, Calcutta,1988, pp. 325 – 372.
16. Shib Shankar Mitra, Bede Baule in Sundarban Samagra, op. cit, p. 17.
17. Shib Shankar Mitra Sundarbane Arjan Sardar in Sundarban Samagra, op.cit, p. 265.
18. Shib Shankar Mitra, Royal Bengaler Atmakatha in Sundarban Samagra, Calcutta,1988, pp. 390 – 93.
19. Shib Shankar Mitra, Sundarbane Arjan Sardar, op. cit, p.279, Bede Baule, op. cit, pp. 16 – 17.
20. Ibid.
21. Shib Shankar Mitra, Sundarbane Arjan Sardar, op. cit, p. 288. Asim Mukhopadhyay, 'Peasants of Parganas' in A.R. Desai edited Peasants Struggle in India, paper beck edition, New Delhi, 1981, pp. 636 – 7. this deals with the outbreak of the Tebhaga Movement, Also see Arkaprabha Sengupta, 'Sundarbaner Jangaler Ekti Samikhya', Mahasweta Devi (ed.) Bartika, July – September, 1989, pp. 45 – 46.

6

A Study of Environmental Damage in Britain and Bengal during the Nineteenth Century and its Reflections in the Novels of few English and Bengali Authors

Sarmistha Mukherjee

Environment today has become a global watchword. Behavioral scientists, industrial psychologists and recent apostles of Total Quality Management have driven home the paramount importance of safe and healthy environment to attain productivity and social and economic improvement. Acts and processes of ravaging the environment have been largely identified and there has been public outcry against such vandalism. The United Nations and many other international bodies have carried out concerted campaigns at different levels using the print and electronic media to preserve the environment for the future as well as the present. Nearly all governments have come out with legislation to safeguard the environment against unchecked and unethical plunder. Thankfully with all the above efforts there have been a welcome awareness of the necessity to prevent any environmental violation supported by promising improvement in actual condition and in the public attitude to environment.

Until the nineteenth century the economy all over the world was largely agrarian and cottage industry could produce enough for human consumption. The population was largely rural; the townspeople were mainly occupied in wholesale trading and legal, administrative and ecclesiastical professions. The governing social order was feudal based on principles of legitimacy and hierarchy. As both agriculture and cottage industries were largely dependent on primary natural resources there was an inherent tendency to preserve the environment. Also, the limited demands could be met from normal yields of nature (no chemical fertilizers had to be added for multiple harvests). Of course there were aberrations - felling of forest trees for firewood, poaching on game animals for meat. But these could hardly upset the environmental equilibrium.

The advent of industrialization changed the scenario. Successive scientific discoveries and technological inventions in the nineteenth century brought about radical transformations in the methods of production. The increase in population in Europe and the colonization of Asia and Africa by the Europeans provided the necessary markets for these new industries. The synergy of all these events is what is known as the Industrial Revolution - which was spearheaded in Britain. The factory system of production forced large-scale migration to the towns where the factories were located. The production was controlled by the emerging capitalist class and new avenues of occupation, as technocrats and managers, came into existence. The feudal social order was replaced by the capitalist system - the guiding principle being laissez-fairie - wherein ones value was being solely determined by market demand and supply. A huge population of operatives, known as 'hands' or 'working class' or 'proletariat' came into existence. These were generally uprooted people from the villages, who were forced to live in subhuman condition around their place of work. This triggered off a natural human reaction vanguarded by the leftists in the form of trade unions. Their philosophy, as propounded by Marx, predicted an evolutionary change in the social order - the capitalist system to be replaced by a socialist system - with production being controlled by society instead of individuals. The second effect was on environment - both physical and social.

The factory system in many cases used mineral as resources, made use of artificial means of production (as boilers, inorganic chemicals), used cantankerous machinery and disposed of a lot of artificial waste all of which caused air, water, heat and sound pollution. Added to these were the unhygienic slums of the workers, lacking in sanitation and cleanliness. In short, the Industrial Revolution proved to be an environmental mess.

Engels, in his 'Condition of Working Class in England', had described in vivid details the squalid and putrid living condition of the workmen during the Industrial Revolution in England. He had strongly emphasized the environmental catastrophe brought about by unchecked and unlegislated industrialization and had given enough statistics to corroborate the deleterious effects of unhealthy environment on the English working class. On the British capital of London he had expounded thus: "*two and half million pair of lungs, two hundred and* fifty thousand fires, crowded *upon an* area three to *four miles* square, consume an enormous amount *of* oxygen, *which* is replaced with difficulty, because the *method* of building cities in itself impedes *ventilation*."[1] His description of a canal in Bolton is a typical example of ecological mess: "a *dark-coloured body* of water, *which* leaves the beholder *in doubt whether* it is a brook or a *wrong string* of stagnant *poodles,* flows *through the town and contributes its share to the* total pollution *of* the air, by no means *pure* without it"[2] In another instance he cites a lane in Manchester where *"inhabitants can pass in and out only by passing through foul pools* of *stagnant* urine *and* excrement".[3] One can imagine the depths to which human existence can succumb owing to unhygienic environment. Industrial England in those times is truly portrayed in the words of Engels – "the cottages are old, dirty, *and* one of the smallest sort, the streets uneven, fallen into ruts *and* in part without drains or pavement; masses of refuge, offal and *sickening* filth lie among standing pools in all directions; the atmosphere is *poisoned by* the effluvia from these, and laden *and darkened by* the smoke of a *dozen* tall factory chimneys".[4] This single sentence summarizes the pollution caused by unregulated industrialization and the exploitation of the working class depriving them of a healthy environment.

We now turn our attention to Bengal. The transition in England in the nineteenth century was from feudalistic to capitalistic social pattern with the advent of industrialization. India was handicapped by her colonial yoke. The industrialization in India was not sponsored by native entrepreneurs but by her colonial masters. The primary aim was to exploit the natural resources of the sub-continent to feed the British industry and populace. Such a skewed industrialization cannot bring about an Industrial revolution and did not develop a potential home-market. The native entrepreneurs gradually followed their British masters and invested in industry but they were subject to control by their colonial overlords thus facing unfair competition. The limited market in India was also not conducive to the growth of large-scale industries and even the native industries in India had to look for markets abroad. Added to this, the inherently indolent Indian bourgeoisie (the major reason for their abject submission to the British) could not come out with any startling scientific discovery or technical innovation that had spearheaded the Industrial Revolution in Britain. For these very practical reasons, India, before her Independence, could not have a balanced industrial development and even now is at the mercy of multi-nationals who decide on major issues on production in the Indian factories. In this context I would like to add that many skilled artisans working in British factories in the nineteenth and early twentieth centuries had proved to be successful and innovative entrepreneurs and had developed an original industrial culture - limited by their formal education - in the town of Howrah. Fakir Mistry had invented the sugar-cane crusher found in every street corner in India. Even now, workmen in Howrah call the common machine part 'punch' as 'panchu'. But sadly speaking, this original Indian technical culture has not permeated or encompassed the modern branches of engineering leaving a country of one billion to look towards multi-nationals for economic and productive technologies. Obviously, in such a scenario, beggars cannot be choosers and in many cases potentially environmentally unsafe industries have been setup in India (as for instance the Union Carbide Plant in Bhopal). The tradition has continued from our colonial past to the present day under the euphemism of 'globalization'.

One of the most disturbing effects of industrialization in India had been the dislocation brought about in the populace. As industrial goods inundated the Indian market a large number of rural weavers and artisans were thrown out of employment and forced to migrate to industrial centers looking for a living. The industrial centers were also few - under the British these were mainly focused in the cities of Calcutta, Bombay, Madras and Cawnpore. But India is a large country with a hugely diverse population with different languages and cultures. This industrial migration thus caused uprooting of the labour-force from own traditional homeland and settlement in the above industrial hubs. This resulted in a cultural friction between the migrant population and the local people. Unlike USA, the Indian cities never proved to be 'melting pots' and urban India still suffers from this inherent sense of division. Even after more than a hundred years, there had been the Shiv Sena riots in Bombay against all migrant population in the city. In most cases it has been found that the urban population live in ghettos distinct from the local people and do not contribute to the social and cultural mainstream of the cities even after few generations. In later years, particularly in independent India, they have vote banks to sustain vested political interest. This, in my opinion, has been a major social failure owing to industrialization in India. The fruits of industrialization has been confined of the elite classes only and fringe benefits have percolated to both the rural and urban proletariat.

Looking at the living conditions of Indian workers, we find they were no better than the description of Engels in his monumental work 'The *Condition of* the *Working Class in England'*. In her book 'The *Working Class in Bengal*'. Deepika Basu writes that the uprooted peasants and artisans who crowded the industrial towns for jobs were herded together in low, dark, ill-ventilated and ill-conserved 'bustees' near the mills, which were not for human habitation. A British Special Inspector for factories Mr. C.A. Walsh had observed "a collection of filthy hovels meets the eye, constructed rudely of mud, thatched with grass or kerosene oil tins flattened out, devoid of drainage and too crowded for a proper supply of air. It remains a marvel how human life, however accustomed to in sanitary surroundings, can survive"[5] Regretfully, such conditions still exist in India. Added to the above woes, 'bustees' were erected below the road level forcing people to sleep on the ground level, that was highly injurious to health. Epidemics of cholera, malaria were very common, which proved to be dangerous not only for the workers but also for the entire town.

Right from the inception, low manufacturing cost and improvised technology provided the competitive edge for Indian industry and these were emphasized by both the Indian and European owners. The Indian industry for more than a century lacked all awareness of Quality Activity and Human Resource Development. As it had been noted in Japan and the West, industry could only flourish with the principles of Total Quality Management that insists on empowered workers and a healthy environment. The need for a pollution free work-place has been acknowledged worldwide and enforced by legislation. For such measures major capital sanctions are needed but the obsession for maintaining low manufacturing cost summarily overruled any such sanction. One case in point is the sprawling foundries of Howrah that has been the major source of low cost casting not only for India but the whole world. It was only after the recent promulgation by the green bench of the Supreme Court that the foundries in Howrah adapted pollution control measures. For decades the foundry workers and in general the people living around the foundries had suffered from premature lung illness, dermatological problems and stomach ailments owing to polluted atmosphere and water.

The above paragraphs have outlined the environmental effects of Industrial revolution in Britain in the nineteenth century and during the colonial industrialization of India following at its heel. We shall now try to look into contemporary literature both in Britain and India and critically evaluate how these prosaic figures have been metaphorically presented. It is well known that statistics and essays are written by and aimed at professionals and experts. One needs a formal training both to compile such data and to understand it for any further action. Hence the readership is limited and fails to create any public outcry. In many cases such documentary work may not be intelligible to the very victims of the social maladies being highlighted. In certain instances the writings have distinct political overtones and are propagandist in nature lacking the natural spontaneity of awareness caused by popular literature. Certainly, once the skeletal data is covered by human flesh and blood in the form of a novel or play, it has a sensitive appeal that reaches beyond all barriers of profession and expertise. A well-written novel on social issues can make the reader identify himself with the characters and the problems become intrinsic instead of remaining extrinsic when propagated politically.

In Britain the most pioneering and effective author to illustrate the ravishment of environment with all its psychic effect caused the Industrial Revolution had been Charles Dickens. He had an ambivalent attitude towards industrialization - looking with a sense of wonder at the speed and prosperity ushered in by the industry and a sense of outrage at the emotional and spiritual damage caused by it. Thus he had characterized the age as: "it was the best of times, it was the worst of times, it was the age of wisdom, it was the age of foolishness ... it was the spring of hope, it was the winter of despair."[6] Dickens had been born and spent his early childhood in pastoral English country-side and he had suffered a sense of shock and loss at the ravaging of the natural environment of his boyhood owing to the rapid industrialization and urbanization of England. He could not accept the total absence of natural variety in industrial surroundings and industrial mechanization was to him never a substitute for the rural setting he had experienced in his early youth. Thus he laments for the workers of Coketown (the factory town in his novel '*Hard Times*') : "wearisome heads (of steam engines) went up and down at the same rate, in hot weather and cold, wet weather and dry, fair weather and foul. The measured motion of their shadows on the walls was the substitute Coketown had to show for the shadows of rustling woods: while for the summer hum of the insects, it could offer, all the year round, from the dawn of Monday to the night of Saturday, the whirr of shafts and wheels." [7]

The two most outstanding features of Dickens' writings were that he had written from first hand experience lending a strong contextual fabric to his novels and in his attempt to explore the psychic effects of industrialization he had used the environment as a metaphor. To him the defilement of nature caused by unchecked industrialization was a torment on the human soul itself. In his description of the image of a dense black cloud hanging over the city in '*Dombey and Son*' (*47th* chapter) Dickens perceives an emotional obscurity that impedes one from knowing the minds of his fellow beings and even his own. As if amoral industrialization, disregarding nature, stifles the Socratic epithet "Know Thyself".

Dickens' *Hard Times* (1854) is a masterpiece as the fully developed study of industrial England. The poignant description of the imaginary Coketown bears testimony to it:

"It (Coketown) was a town of red brick, or of brick that would have been red if the smoke and ashes allowed it; but as matters stood it was a town of unnatural red and black like the painted face of a savage. It was a town of machinery and tall chimneys, out of which interminable serpents of smoke trailed themselves for ever and ever, and never got uncoiled. It had a black canal in it, and a river that run purple with ill smelling dye, and vast piles of building full of windows where the piston of the steam engine worked monotonously up and down like the head of an elephant in a state of melancholy madness." [8]

In a single paragraph Dickens has depicted the miseries from air, water and noise pollution caused by industry. This he expresses with his intense similies as "interminable serpents" for the coiling smoke coming out from the engine exhausts. The entire process of industrialization to him is "an elephant in a state of melancholy madness" - as if nature has been ravished by a mad elephant. Dickens continues with this elephant metaphor throughout the novel. At one stage he even uses the infernal metaphor for the whole of Coketown – "seemed to frying in oil" [9]. The effect on the inhabitants he portrays as "stokers emerged from low underground doorways into factory yards, and sat on steps, and posts, and palings, wiping their swarthy visages, and contemplating coals." [10] Dickens pities the Coketown workers for the environmental void in their lives; forcible substitution of natural environment by inhuman mechanization has left them with only vision of black coal!

Even in the arid landscape of industrial England Dickens seeks solace in the freshness of early mornings when the "mad elephants" are yet to rattle their ugly heads. The flush of dawn is a dichotomy - a saving grace from the repulsive day. This he pours out in the musings of Stephen Blackpool as he departs from Coketown early in the morning:

"So strange to turn from the chimneys to the birds, so strange to have road dust on his feet instead of coal grit, so strange to have lived to his time of life, and yet to be beginning like a boy this summer morning!"[11]

Dickens persists with his sense of outrage at the effacing of natural surroundings with a missionary zeal in a number of his novels. With a commendable foresight he had envisaged that the uprooting of people from nature and confining them by vocation to polluting industries and by habitation to unhealthy slums would stifle their human spirit and would need remedial action for convalescence. This is what the world in general has realized by hindsight. The following paragraph from *Old Curiosity Shop* (1840) gives a touching description of ecological ruin in England of his times:

"A long suburb of red brick houses - some with patches of green-ground, where coal dust, and factory smoke darkened the shrinking leaves and coarse rank flowers, and where the struggling vegetation sickened and sank under the hot breath of kiln and furnace."[12]

His use of metaphors is pertinent – "the dark depressing influence stole upon their spirits."[13] To him the tall chimneys pouring out their "plague of smoke" are a "horror of oppressive dreams".[14] So to Dickens this industrialization seems to be a nightmare; but in his writing there is a streak of hope that the horrible dream would one day come to an end. The emphasis wrought upon the human spirit is analogous to "dismantled houses here and there blackened desolate but yet inhabited". [15]

Another notable author who had concentrated on the social issues arising out of industrialization in England was Elizabeth Gaskell. Though not as emphatic and illustrative as Dickens on environmental changes, she too cannot totally ignore it in her novels. In '*North and South*'; her famous novel on industrial relation and class reconciliation, we find the reference to the imaginary town of Milton as where one "must endure smoke and fogs". The heroine of the novel, who has migrated to Milton from the pastoral South of England is shocked to find that she has to wash her hands thrice every morning to combat the dirt. The greater shock is the chance meeting with a girl of her own age who had contracted a terminal disease owing to unhygienic working condition in a cotton mill. The poor girl says in despair "there's many one as works in a carding-room, that falls into a waste, coughing and spitting blood, because they're just poisoned by the fluff". And she is outraged at the cynical attitude of the mill-owners regarding public health and hygiene as reflected in the conversation she had with one of them that he has implemented the pollution control device because the fuel economy achieved thereby paid for the investment.

In her other novel *Mary Burton* Mrs. Gaskell had been more radical in portraying the social tribulations of the working class. Her exposure of the social degeneracy caused by the ruthless factory culture of Manchester is poignant. The novel of hers can certainly be called a milestone in the analysis of the debauchery brought about in the lives of simple English womenfolk who were forced to migrate to the factory towns from rural settings. Whereas we have Bessy Higgins physically suffering from her exposure to industry in *North and South*, we find Esther in *Mary Burton* who has her morals polluted by the heartless industrial environment. The novel Mary Barton curiously opens with a typical Dickensian prologue - the contrast between the pastoral country side and the smoky, dirty factory town with a yearning for the lost greenery. Coincidentally, the Bengali novel *Koilakuthir Deshe* by

Shailajananda Mukhopadhyay also opens with the description of blackening of the original saffron soil in the coal mining districts of Bengal. The novel describes the shifting environment, both physical and social, caused by the mining operations with touching scenes of migration to the towns during market peaks and back to the surrounding villages during recession.

Now let us come to the ground realities of the 19th century England - the real life effects of Dickens' metaphor. Robert Owen had demonstrated that other models of industrial and urban development were possible, and that they were economically viable too, but they made little impression on other industrialists whose economic ambitions were rarely checked by the humane need to create a decent or civilized environment: It had been said that every novel of Dickens had initiated corrective legislation in Britain. We find that a Public Health Act was passed by Parliament in 1848 followed by the Sanitary Act of 1866. Little actual progress had been achieved by these Acts and the 'The Great Stink" of the Thames in 1858, described by Disraeli as "a Stygian pool reeking with ineffable and intolerable horrors", had made the Parliament to react also. The Royal Commission of 1869 investigated the problems of public health once again. It declared that among things "necessary for civilized social life" were good water supplies and proper drainage, the removal of nuisances (including smoke) healthy houses, clean street, the inspection of food, and the provision of adequate burial ground. This led in 1871 to the creation of Local Government Board with responsibility, among other matters, for public health. In 1874 Disraeli was elected Prime Minister and in 1875 his government passed another Public Health Act. This consolidated various laws and regulations on public health into a single code on which sanitary law has been based ever since.

In India the Factory Act was introduced in 1881 with statutes on health, safety and welfare of the workers but all along there has been a general apathy towards such legislation, which has been only taken in letter and never really in spirit either by the mill-owners or the political leadership. The British were hardly concerned about the Indian working class (as expected) and a broad section of the Indian Nationalist Movement was afraid that factory legislation would retard the growth of native Indian capitalism. The cunning exemption of the British owned mills from the Factory Act corroborated this suspicion of the Indian elite. The youthful intelligentsia was more concerned about political freedom from the British than about the damage wrought upon physical and social environment by unchecked industrialization. Hence the need of maintaining a safe and healthy environment along with the development of industry lacked realization among Indians and remained a neglected topic for long. It was only after independence that Indians reacted to this issue and a gradual awareness fermented in the country. One may compare this to the classic cartoon in the *Punch* imagazine (12 July, 1855) which was published when Mr. Faraday himself had highlighted the pollution in the water of the river Thames in *Times* (9 July, 1855). This clearly shows how the scientific community in Britain had reacted to environmental damage in the early days of Industrial Revolution. As a sequel to this initiative taken by Faraday a Bill was enacted in 1858 by the House of Commons to clear up the "Stygian pool reeking with ineffable and intolerable horrors." (Disraeli's words as he addressed to the House of commons).

Notes and References

1. Frederick Engels : *The Condition of the Working Class in England*, p. 394.
2. Ibid : pp. 345-346.
3. Ibid : p. 351.
4. Ibid : p. 361.
5. Annual Report on the Working of the Factories Act in Bengal, 1894.

   Gen. Misc., 13-34, July 1895 quoted from Deepika Basu 'The Working Class in Bengal'.
6. A Tale of Two Cities, Book I, Chapter 1, p. 3.
7. *Hard Times*, Book II, Chapter 1, p. 86.
8. *Hard Times*, Book I, Chapter 5, p. 22.
9. *Hard Times*, Book II, Chapter 1, p. 86.

10. *Hard Times*, Book II, Chapter 1. p. 86.
11. *Hard Times*, Book II, Chapter 6, p. 124.
12. *Old Curiosity* Shop, Book II, Chapter XLV pp. 335-336.
13. *Old Curiosity Shop,* Book II, Chapter XLV pp. 335-336.
14. *Old Curiosity Shop,* Book II, Chapter XLV pp. 335-336.
15. *Old Curiosity Shop,* Book II, Chapter XLV pp. 335-336.

Bibliography

1. Karl Marx and Frederick Engels, collected works, vol. 4, Progress Publishers, Moscow, 1975.
2. Deepika Basu, *The working class in Bengal : Formative years*, K.P. Bagchi & Co, Kolkata/Delhi, First Publication 1993, Present Publication 1995.
3. C.P. Hill, British Economic and Social History 1700-1982, Edward Arnold (Publishers) Limited.
4. Charles Dickens, *Hard Times*, A Norton Critical Edition, Edited by George Form and Sylvere Momod, 1st Edition 1966, 2nd Edition 1990.
5. Charles Dickens, *A Tale of two cities*, Wordsworth Editions Limited, 1993.
6. Charles Dickens, Dombey and Stons, Wordsworth Editions Ltd., 1995.
7. Charles Dickens, *Old Curiosity Shop*, Oxford University Press, 1960.
8. Elizabeth Gaskell, *North and South*, Penguin Popular Classics, 1994.
9. Elizabeth Gaskell, *Mary Burton*, Penguin English Library, 1970.
10. Herbert L. Sussinan, *Victorians and the Machine*, Harvard University Press, 1968.
11. Malcolm Andrews, *Dickens on England and the English*, Sussex, Harvester, 1979.

7

Artistic Impressions of the Famine and Environment : A Case Study of the Bengal Famine (1943)

Keka Dutta Roy

With the great impact of the Second World War, perceptible social, political and economic changes made inroads into the lives of the Bengalees. The war aggravated the exhaustion of popular forces : it also led to acute discontented occasional and sporadic near-revolutionary outbreaks. Though India was spared of actual military devastation, mass suffering was acute, for war meant rampant inflation, widespread corruption, shortages, black marketeering and eventually a famine in 1943 of a magnitude unknown in the history of eastern India since 1770.[1]

In 1943, the whole of the then Bengal with parts of Eastern Bihar and Northern Orissa was in the throes of a famine. Recent researches have confirmed the perceptions of the concerned contemporaries that this was a 'man-made' famine. The worse affected areas were Tamluk and Contai in Midnapore, Diamond Harbour in South West Bengal, the districts of Chittagong, Dacca, Faridpur, Tippera and Noakhali. In 1942, a cyclone and accompanying tidal wave swept the entire coast of West Bengal and North Orissa resulting in loss of crops, destruction of property and loss of lives. Shortfalls in foodgrains production for two consecutive years and stoppage of rice imports from the Japanese occupied Burma were aggravated by the grain purchases of the vastly expanded allied army stationed in Eastern India, the Denial Policy (that shifted all means of normal transport from civilian operations and placed them at the disposal of the army and the government) and finally hoarding of foodgrains by the traders sent the prices of foodgrains sky rocketing. So the gradual decline in the per capita availability of rice along with an inefficient grain-marketing system was the cause for the famine.[2]

The situation was aggravated by gross mismanagement and deliberate profiteering. The worst sufferers were the landless labourers, the share-croppers, the small and the marginal farmers of the rural areas, the petty non-foodgrain traders and the self-employed lower-middle-class of both the rural and urban areas. Apart from the big traders and the industrialists, fixed job holding urban classes and workers from the formal sector were untouched by the famine, they became the beneficiaries of the newly introduced urban rationing system and the dearness allowance instituted to offset the price rise. Peasants died in millions while workers from the informal sector and the self employed died in thousands.[3]

In the terrible summer and autumn of 1943, 3 lakhs of people from the neighbourhood trekked to Calcutta to starve to death on its streets begging no longer for rice but for the water in which rice was cooked. Picking of food from dustbins, eating of rotten food, were common sights. Mass feeding by charitable organisations through relief kitchens started in July '43 but these attempts were inadequate. Destitutes died in streets. Starvation and malnutrition led to major epidemics of malaria, enteric-fever, cholera, small pox, dysentry and diarrhoea. Somnath Hore an artist of the time recalls "the worse affected were the potters, barbers, washermen, fishermen and the landless. Their womenfolk were often lured away by touts to service the soldiers. Some women came back from the street of the towns riddled with veneral disease. Without food or medical care they were dying". A large number of people lived in the rural areas on charity but that form of charity also dried up. There was a break up of so many homes, there was snapping of so many family-ties. Society, relatives, family, all were forgotten. While small-land holders, landless labourers and coastal poor turned destitutes in rural areas. Old men, women of all ages and children formed the majority among the destitutes of Calcutta.[4] Even Sir John Woodhead, the Chairman of the Famine Inquiry Commission later remarked : "It has been for us a sad task to enquire into the course and causes of the Bengal famine. We have been haunted by a deep sense of tragedy. A million and a half of the poor of Bengal fell victim to circumstances for which they themselves were not responsible. Society, together with its organs failed to protect its weaker members. Indeed, there was a moral and social breakdown as well as an administrative breakdown."

The horrors of the Bengal famine shook the very basis of the old values of humanism. These were the dark days for Bengal. It was a compelling situation to forge a cultural revolution. An anguished but creative response to the famine came from the very classes which survived the holocaust.[5]

Sufferings of the victims did evoke a serious response from eminent writers. They expressed their feelings through their work.[6] The poet Sukanta Bhattacharya wrote in his famous poem-

ঐতিহাসিক ঃ ‘একদা দুর্ভিক্ষ এল
ক্ষুধার ক্ষমাহীন তাড়নায়
পাশাপাশি ঘেঁষা ঘেঁষি সবাই দাঁড়ালে একই লাইনে
ইতর-ভদ্র, হিন্দু আর মুসলমান,
একই বাতাসে নিলে নিঃশ্বাস।’

The Bengal famine was the catalyst for the full blossoming of Tarasankar Bandyopadhyay's creative potentials as a novelist. The famine of 1943 was used as a backdrop in his famous " মন্বন্তর " (Manwantar) and in many of his stories and novels, he reflected on the break up of family life due to economic stress resulting out of the famine. The pangs of hunger, could be felt when Gunada Babu's wife said in মন্বন্তর :

"টাকার আর কোন দাম নেই আমার কাছে। আজ তিন দিন ঘরে চাল নেই। তিন দিন আগে নীচের পানওয়ালা কিউয়ে দাঁড়িয়ে চাল এনে আমাকে দিয়েছিল। পরে শুনলাম লোকটার নিজের ঘরে হাঁড়ি চাপেনি। তাই আর তার কাছে নিইনি। ছোট ছেলেটা তো-ভাত-ভাত করে দিন রাত চিৎকার করছে।"

Manik Bandyopadhyay in his stories like 'Aaj Kaal Porshur Galpa' and 'Nichu Chokhe Meyeli Samasya' harped the case of prostitution or the uncertain condition of the contemporary female society.

Bibhuti Bhushan Bandyopadhyay depicted the famine in his revealing novel "Ashani Sanket" or "Distant Thunder". Bengal faced such a great famine that it generated strong grief and emotion in the minds of the writers of Bengal" he said. Sporadic outburst were envinced in the creative writings of Achintya Sengupta, Subodh Ghosh, Subhas Mukhopadhyay, Abul Mansur Ahmed, Rameshwar Chandra Sen and others who were deeply moved by the famine.[8]

It was this famine that revolutionalized the Bengal stage through the production of Bijon Bhattacharya's 'Navanna', which was a story of the grievous Bengal Famine and how it wrecked a peasant family of Midnapore. It was a domestic tragedy presented in broad social perspective. Its aim was to confront the social issues and to protest against some social wrongs and to make one think about them.[9] It was the immediate cause that launched the IPTA and The Anti-Fascist Writers and Artists Association with direct and tacit support of most of the well known intellectuals, writers, artists, actors, dancers, musicians and film makers who played a crucial role in making Indian music, dance and theatre both in a social and formal sense. The famine was one of the factors in the establishment of the Calcutta group of painters and sculptures in 1943 who interpreted the new visual languages and techniques of European modernists with Indian sensibilities and contemporary awareness of the human situation in India. The barbarity and heartlessness all around induced pioneer artists of the group like Nirode Mazumdar, Subho Tagore, Gopal Ghosh, Paritosh Sen, Rathin Moitra, Prankrishna Pal, Pradosh Dasgupta, Ramkinkar, Sunil Madhav Sen and others to inspire a new ideology by creating a new synthesis between the east and the west. The Bengal famine helped this group in augmenting the resurgence of a new art movement to raise a voice of protest against the prevalent art situation of the Bengal School of Art, which produced painting on literacy and mythological themes and western academism in a naturalistic style of art employed mostly for portrait. This is not to deny that Rabindranath Tagore, Gaganendanath Tagore, Jamini Roy and some artists, of the Kala Bhavan Viswabharati, like Nandalal Bose, Benode Behari Mazumdar had been trying to break new grounds in content and style. However the first organised collective effort to challenge the Bengal School came from the Calcutta Group, who viewed art in its international content, explored the modern styles developed in the west and above all showed a concern for man and society. Most of the group artists were driven to the periphery of the philosophy of communism and were close to the cultural front of the communist party.[10]

However the Calcutta Group did not include painters like Zainul Abedin, Chittoprosad Bhattacharya, Somnath Hore and Debabrata Mukhopadhyay who came to limelight by working on the famine itself. The famine had indeed stimulated the arts in such a soul-stirring manner. Most of the creative artists to be so stirred were from the urban middle classes.[11]

Chittoprasad Bhattacharya joined the political life at a time of great upheaval at national and international levels when the struggle for independence was entering its final stages. World economic crisis was getting acute and during the Bengal Famine, Chittoprosad toured the countryside of Bengal extensively and reported the human predicament in black and white under the title "Hungry Bengal".[12]

Although Chittoprosad was not formally a member of the communist party, he was welcomed into the fold of the party by its secretary P.C. Joshi who let Chittoprosad choose his own way and to serve the party's cause without let or hindrance. Chittoprosad would go from one famine ravaged village to another. From one gruel kitchen to the other, from one rural grain market to another village "haat" drawing sketches which would be published in the Bengali Weekly "Janayuddha" and the English Weekly "The People's War" of the communist party. Chittoprosad drew from direct experience of the people's struggle and suffering. There was not a single political line of struggle which could evade his attention. Chittoprosad made a promising start as a print maker with colour and monochrome wood-cuts but his famine-sketches were stylistically narrative in style with images rendered in an abbreviated academic naturalism in which lines played a strong role and had a gestural expression. From that, Chittoprosad opted for a folk-based formation with a social content. The works of Chittoprosad thus bear a close resemblance to that of Pata painting tradition of Bengal group and figures are well knit into a compact composition.[13]

The true significance of Chittoprosad's work lay in his deep and profound understanding of the suffering and struggle of the ordinary Indian people and also the knowledge and command over the cultural traditions to which he belonged. Chittoprosad along with a few artists faced the greater social reality of his time and painted them with natural ease, power and conviction. Chittoprosad was soon asked by the editors of the papers to cover Midnapore in the way he had covered Chittagong and it now fell upon Somnath Hore, a young communist artist and activist to do the usual reporting from Chittagong.[14]

As a urban youth, Somnath Hore started his career as a relief worker and an artist journalist of the communist party. He started his art career doing posters for this purpose and this led him to be excited about art. During the Bengal famine, he was involved in the people's relief committee in Chittagong. In the course of his work, he came in touch with Chittoprosad and followed his path.[15] The will for minimal animal living and its denial, the physical suffering of the humiliated underdog of humanity on the one hand and the vile display of the might of the inflictors of the wounds made Somnath a political artist.

The earliest of Somnath's visual reportages were three sketches published in "Janayudha" in 1944. The sketches were followed by a deluge of sketches done on spot and life drawings meant to serve as reportages of the famine. These were scenes with hapless victims of famine, suffering and dying peasants, sick and infirm destitutes and portraits of peasants. All these were live drawings definitional lines following representational contours producing anatomical drawings.[16]

In Somnath's works, elements were very real as and when he experienced them during the famine when he presented them in his drawings and sketches: these assumed almost symbolic qualities parts standing for the whole. Somnath's human and animal figures were almost skeletal with prominent thorax appearing as a cage of ribs with each rib jutting out prominently. The children who would invariably be there in most of Somnath's drawings would have out of proportion malarial spleens, their heads would be enormous skulls with small bony face perched on rickety torsos.[17]

For Somnath, whose visual arts centred round the famine it was only very natural to be attracted towards Zainul Abedin who was then by far the most perceptive of all artists on the famine.[18]

Zainul Abedin was a romantic interpreter of the natural environment. He was a non-political individual : a mere artist of nature. But the Bengal Famine of 1943-a case of terrible human exploitation and degradation transformed the peace loving romantic young landscape painter from East Bengal into a rebel and an agitating protestor for the rest of his life. Soon after the famine had broken out, Zainul went to his home in Mymensingh. The ghastly scenes almost paralysed him and he returned to Calcutta. But the destitutes came with him. At Calcutta in 1943, humanity was at its most ignominious condition competing with dogs in their hunt for a meal out of the garbage tins on pavements. Zainul then 29, was severely shocked but he tried to control his emotions and began to sketch the nightmarish scenes.[19] The picture of destitution, hunger, decay and death was forcibly projected through a series of monochromatic drawings done between 1943-45. He could not get away from the academic naturalistic convention but his choice of motif the stark juxtaposition on black and homographic characterization were telling and the pointed lines had gestural quality which the expressionists would recognise as the objective expressions of deeply felt experience.

A young art teacher of small earnings, it had become very difficult for him to procure quality art materials. So he made drawings in black ink with dry brush tinted with yellow and pink on grey packaging boards. He recorded the famine scenes with documentary objectivity and after viewing Zainul's famine sketches, Sarojini Naidu had said 'They are more in their poignant appeal than the most eloquent and impassioned words'.[20]

As truthful records of the history of Bengal in 1943, Abedin's drawings are invaluable documents. As a worshipper of beauty in the terrible phases of human life Zainul raised the famine sketches to an art of social commentary and artistic excellence. Thus, with his famine sketches, Zainul became the first important Bengali artist of social realism and an artist of the downtrodden.[21]

Zainul Abedin worked for the cause of humanism and socialism. It was not without some commitment that Zainul participated in the famine. His heart would bleed at the sorrows, sufferings, pangs and agonies of the toiling masses whom he falt as his own.[22]

Debabrata Mukhopadhyay was a well known communist artist of the time whose visuals were seen through posters, cartoons and illustrations of the contemporary writers. [23] His sister Mrinalini Dasgupta recalls in a reminiscing article :

"৪৩-এর প্রথমে দিকে দুর্ভিক্ষের করাল ছায়া নামল। চারিদিকেই ক্রন্দন। হাওড়া, শেয়ালদা স্টেশনে হাঁটতে গেলে মৃতদেশের পাশ দিয়ে আসতেই হয়। মনটা কেমন দুমড়ে মুচড়ে গেছে। একদিন আমাদের বাড়িতে কোনও খাবার নেই টাকাও নেই। বড়দার (দেবব্রত মুখোপাধ্যায়) মাহিনা, আমার মাহিনা সব শেষ। বড়দাকে তা জানালাম। বড়দা একটু গম্ভীর হয়ে পরক্ষণেই বলল আমার এক

বন্ধুর বইয়ের মলাটে আঁকার কাজ করেছিলাম, দেখি কিছু পাই কিনা। আমি বসেই আছি। বেলা ১২টা বাজে। বাড়িতে খাবার লোক পাঁচ জন ..... শুধুই ভাবছি আর ভাবছি। ৪৩ সালে আরও অনেক বিপদের মাঝ দিয়ে গিয়েছি, কিন্তু ও দিনের বিপদ ও এ সময়ে বড়দার পরিচয় আজও স্মৃতির অক্ষয় হয়ে আছে। বড়দা ফিরে এল বেলা বারোটার পরে। একটু চিন্তা বা উদ্বেগের রেখা মাত্র নেই তার মুখে। আমি ব্যস্ত হয়ে এগিয়ে গিয়ে হাত পাতলাম। সে একটু ক্ষরিকের জন্য ম্রিয়মান হয়ে হেসেই উত্তর দিল। না রে কিছুই নেই। দশটা টাকা পেলাম কিন্তু সিঁড়ির মুখেই মাস্টার মশাই (প্রতিবেশী) দেবু বাবু বললেন দশটা টাকা দিতে পারেন, ছেলেটার পাঁচদিন জ্বর। আজ ডাক্তার ডাকলাম, কিন্তু ওষুধ পথ্যের টাকা নেই। আমি সামনের মাসেই দিয়ে দেব। তাই টাকাটা ওকেই দিয়ে দিলাম .... কিছু হবে না। সামনের দোকান থেকে কিছু তেলে ভাজা আর মুড়ি নিয়ে আসি আর এতেই আমাদের হয়ে যাবে। বড়দার নিরুত্তাপ এইরকম ব্যক্তিত্ব আমি কম দেখেছি।"

Such was the drastic change in the social environment, the political thinking and the economy that its profound influence was decisively felt on the Indian artistic scenario.[24]

The artists were thoroughly shaken by the famine death and the moral degradation that followed. In fact it stirred the soul of the new creative artists of Bengal obsessively. Such was the choice of art of this period that one would recognise them as having an objective expression of a deeply felt experience. Artists welcomed the need to develop art with sensibility, having relevance to the changed circumstances. In short, artists were interested in the immediate environment of the time.[25]

Notes and References

1. Prodosh Dasgupta, The Calcutta Group : its aims and achievements, Lalit Kala Contemporary 31 and Sumit Sarkar, Modern India, Delhi, 1983.
2. Pranab Ranjan Roy, 'Hunger and the Painter : Somnath Hore and the wounds' in Somnath Hore : Bronzes, CIMA, Calcutta, 1995 and Paul Greenough, Prosperity and Misery in modern Bengal, New York, 1982 and Peoples War, June, 1945.

3. Pranab Ranjan Roy, op. cit. and Amartya Sen 'Famine Mortality : "A study of the Bengal Famine 1943' in E. Hobsbawm (ed.) Peasants in History, Delhi, 1980.
4. Famine Inquiry Commission Report on Bengal, New Delhi,1984 and Somnath Hore, 'wounds' in CIMA, op. cit. and Statesman, 16th October, 1943.
5. Prodosh Dasgupta, op. cit., Sukanta Bhattacharya in his Poem 'Sukanto Samagro', Calcutta ,1979.
6. Sukanta Bhattacharya in his Poem 'ঐতিহাসিক' 'Sukanto Samagro', Calcutta, 1979.
7. Tarasankar Bandyopadhyay, (Bengali) Tarasankar Rachanavali volume 5, and vol. 20, Calcutta, 1404 B.S.
8. Manik Bandyopadhyay, Manik Granthavali, vol. 6, Calcutta, 1982, and Bhudev Chaudhuri, Bangla Sahityer Chhoto Galpo O Galpokar, Calcutta, 1962 and Bibhuti Bithika, Calcutta, 1975.
9. Anuradha Roy, Panchaser Manwantar O Banglar Shilpa Sahitya, Anustup, 1989 and Itihas Anusandhan, Vol. 2.
10. Prodosh Dasgupta, op. cit.
11. Anuradha Roy, op. cit. and Pranab Ranjan Roy, op. cit.
12. E. Alkazi edited Art Heritage, Vol. 5, New Delhi, 1985-86 and Pranab Ranjan Roy, 'To carry the roots in the venus', in Lalit Kala Contemporary 24 and 25.
13. Ibid.
14. Ibid.
15. Somnath Hore in 'Wounds' op. cit. and Pranab Ranjan Roy 'Hunger and the Painter Transactions' Vol. I, no. 2, 1981, Cressida and Jaya Appaswamy, 'The Graphic art of Somnath Hore' in Lalit Kala Contemporary 11 and Lalit Kala Contemporary 24, op. cit.
16. Ibid.
17. Ibid.
18. Ibid.
19. Mohammad Sirajul Islam and Zainul Abedin, Vol. I, Art of Bangladesh Series and Peoples War, February 25, 1945 and Lalit Kala Contemporary 24, op. cit.
20. Ibid.
21. Ibid.
22. Ali Matlub, Amader Zainul, Dacca, 1985.
23. Interview with the artist.

24. 'মুখর' সাহিত্য পত্রিকা, দেবব্রত মুখোপাধ্যায় সংখ্যা, চৈত্র সংখ্যা, ১৯৮৫।
25. Famine Inquiry Commission Report, op. cit. article by Nirode Mazumdar : Art being and relevant to the situation, Lalit Kala Contemporary no. 22.

8

In Search of Football Ground: Development and Problems of Open Space in Twentieth Century Urban Bengal

Kausik Bandyopadhyay

Introduction

In the modern world sport and environment are complexly interrelated phenomena. While environment usually plays a vital role in the shaping of sport's incidents and cultures, the physical geography of sport,[1] in particular, its relationship with the local environment and microclimate[2] remains a decisive factor in sport's popularization and commercialization. This internal fundamental geography of Indian sports in general and of football in particular has been entirely ignored by social scientists. Football ground/ stadium development/ redevelopment, largely and continuously influenced by environmental factors like weather patterns or nature of local landscape, also reflects the emotional attachment, social control, political design and economic transformation of the Indian nation. Beyond this fascinating story of the game's internal geography, however, lies an external factor which is no less interesting either. This refers to the complex equation between the development and problems of *open space*[3] utilization and the question of football's popularity and decline in urban India.

Like a particular sport itself, sports ground may claim to have its own history. The availability, opportunity and utilization of sports space/ground can have a deciding sway on the growth, popularity and decline of a particular sport at a particular place. More importantly, the growth, development and problems of sports ground are intimately related to wider socio-economic, political and cultural processes. The history of football grounds in urban Bengal in the twentieth century helps us unmask the relational complexities between the open space utilization, sports ground development and popularization of sport on the one hand and the broader issues of politics, economy, society and culture on the other. The present essay seeks to analyze the process of growth, development and problems of open space vis-à-vis football ground[4] in twentieth century urban Bengal[5] in a historical perspective and locate the consequent emerging issues and crises in the game's history against the backdrop of political tension, social unrest, economic challenge and cultural conflict.

Open Space and Football Ground in Late Colonial Bengal

Conventional urban history of late colonial Bengal does not offer any concrete ideas about the evolution of open space and its utilization as sports grounds.[6] It seems fairly certain, however, that open space remained in abundance in early twentieth century Bengal. Greater availability and easier reclamation of open space naturally provided suitable option for its use as sports ground. Football as the most popular sport of contemporary Bengal required open grounds for Bengali's indigenous pursuit of the game. In fact, football's social popularization as a mass spectator sport[7] in the first two decades of the twentieth century was well complemented and facilitated by the acquisition of green open spaces for the purpose of football-play throughout the cities of Calcutta and Dacca and their outskirts. Vast open spaces in the suburbs of Calcutta, too, gradually attracted the youth towards playing the game. It was from these suburban towns[8] that the Bengali clubs of Calcutta used to get a rich supply of footballers since the turn of the century. Moreover, football began to enjoy a reasonable edge over other sports like cricket and hockey in the aftermath of Mohun Bagan's historic IFA Shield victory in 1911.[9] Thus, competing claims of other sports were far less. This universal popularity of football made it the staple sport played on those grounds.

In view of abundance of open space, acquisition, maintenance and consolidation of claims on different sports grounds did not seem to be a very complex process in urban Bengal during the late colonial period. The clash between de jure ownership and de facto possession was scarce indeed. Rather, the question of control over these open spaces used as playgrounds might have been a source of conflict among locally influential people. [10] Open space availability, of course, did not necessarily imply its suitability as football ground everywhere. In Calcutta, for example, public voice for a stadium began to be raised from the 1930s onwards. [11] Increasing popularity of football-play as a daily popular pursuit in the unorganized sector, however, certainly owed quite a bit to greater availability of open space and its utilization as football ground. This is not to deny at all the importance of football as a cultural nationalist force [12] that really played the most crucial role in its social popularization in contemporary Bengal. But, that the favoruable balance of open space in the physical environment of late colonial Bengal also played its part in the same process also merits careful attention.

Problems of Open Space and Challenges to Ground Development : Post Colonial Scenario in West Bengal

When India achieved freedom from British yoke, football had already become an integral part of Bengali popular culture. Yet freedom also brought in its wake unfortunate reality of Partition. In that context, football in Bengal came to acquire an ethnic/sub regional dimension through *ghati-Bangal* conflict on the maidan.[13] As a result, the decades of the 1950s and the 1960s witnessed intensive massfication of football in Bengal. This period also experienced major changes in Bengal's urban landscape. These changes emanated mostly from a radical population explosion, hectic industrialization and rapid but somewhat unplanned urbanization. The huge refugee influx from East Pakistan to West Bengal in the aftermath of Partition significantly contributed to these interrelated changes. All this resulted in increasing pressure on open space and a consequent rise in the commercial value of land. Land open spaces came to be used more and more for civic, public as well as commercial purposes such as housing, refugee settlement, slum, sanitation and drainage, public building, governmental office, road, shop, park, car park, temple etc.

The pressure on land in urban Bengal multiplied with a new wave of refugee influx from Bangladesh to West Bengal in the context of Bangladesh War of 1971. Forceful acquisition of fallow/ waste land and open space for residential and other civic purposes became the order of the day. Official civic bodies like corporations and municipalities came to acquire such land to sustain enhancing pressure of population in concerned localities and settlements. Most importantly, the outskirts and suburbs of Calcutta fell to the full thrust of urbanization from the 1970s. The result was gradual but steady contraction of open space, a good quantity of which had hitherto been used as sports/football grounds. In the 1980s-90s, the process of open space contraction reached a new high with a galloping rise in the commercial value of land in urban areas. The process of conversion of open spaces into urban conglomerations of various sorts was accelerated by the steady growth of a 'promoter raj'[14] in and around Calcutta. These promoters, mostly in liaison with political parties, openly forced vast open spaces into house building and commercial complexes. Added to this was the civic bodies' drive to beautify Calcutta and other suburban towns by acquiring most of the remaining small pieces of green open space. The following table shows how sports grounds came under attack from different quarters.

The drastic reduction in the scores of open green space in the last few decades has certainly led to a severe crisis in the maintenance and development of football grounds in urban Bengal, uniquely articulating at the same time power relations at different levels - political, social and economic. A study of the encroachments upon open landscape shows that socio-political power relations play a vital role in the fight for acquisition and possession of such spaces as football ground. The politics of retention of open space as sports/football ground or its reclamation for commercial use

Table -1

Area	*No. of sports ground in 1990*	*Extinct sites (2003) / replaced by*	*Encroached sites (2003) / encroached by*	*Remaining sports grounds (2003)*
Sodepur (Amarabati area - 1 sq. km.)	8	6 / baby school, house, park and sweet shop, shopping complex, temple, housing complex.	1/roadside open space now surrounded houses and used as a dumping ground.	1/a club maintained , by open space reduced size due to the construction of the clubroom.
Barasat (Nabapalli area - road stretch zone of 3 kms.)	9	7/ house, housing complex, shop and connecting roads.	1 / extension of temple.	1 / maintained by a local club.
Basirhat (heartland area - 4 sq. kms.)	11	3 / houses.	-	8/one maintained by the local municipality and the others by local clubs.

involves not only a contest of social and political influences but also criminal activities at times often resulting in law and order problems. It also uncovers the complex history of smaller clubs with special reference to their socio-political support base and economic sustainability in the suburban towns of West Bengal.

Gradual disappearance of open space resulted in a real difficulty in finding playgrounds for children and teenagers in urban areas. This was an imperceptible attack on the supply line of raw recruits who would later become players of merit in the organized sector. In the context of scarcity of open space alia sports ground due to indiscriminate appropriation of land, football as a mass spectator sport suffered most in Bengal since cricket came to lay its competing claims to the existing sports grounds hitherto dominated by football. In the late 1980s and the 1990s, the competitive edge cricket came to enjoy over football in India [15] had its repercussions on Bengali boys and girls. Moreover, the scarcity has become so acute that one small ground has to be used periodically for two sports in rotation and respectively by two or more clubs. Thus, the decline in football's popularity and standard during the past two decades can be partly attributed to this environmental problem, i.e., indiscriminate assault on open space resulting in its speedy disappearance from urban Bengal.

Impact of Open Space Contraction on Bengal Football

Football in Bengal began to experience a slump in terms of both standard and popularity since the early 1980s. This was a result of various factors. The gradual dearth in the production of quality footballers and the failure of the Indian Football Association as well as the major clubs of Calcutta to adapt to the changing pattern of the global game accounted most for its steady deterioration in standard in the 1980s. On the other hand, increasing spectator violence in Calcutta football, [16] live telecast of World Cup and Euro-American football in India,[17] cricket's increasing popularity since India's World Cup victory of 1983 and the game's successful commercialization in the 1990s [18] in contrast to football administration's failure to do that [19] and lack of India's success in international football [20] as well as absence of viable

Indian footballing icons[21] are some of the major factors that led to a steady decline in the popularity and mass base of the game. Yet it is only international cricket that remains most popular in India alia Bengal while domestic football still holds its ground among Bengalis.[22] But the pursuit of the game in urban Bengal suffered a blow owing to a continuous decline in the availability of reasonably good football grounds since the 1970s. Unavailability of playgrounds had the direct impact of depriving different age groups the opportunity to play football from their childhood. Rearing a raw band of future footballers in the unorganized sector was thus nullified in the bud. This social and demographic process of depravity has proved a bane for Bengal football in the long run. To understand the operational aspects and affective dimensions of this complex process, it may be useful here to employ the conceptual models of Y. F. Tuan and the theoretical insights provided by Michel Foucault.

Tuan uses the term the term *topophilia* to describe the deep affection of people towards particular social spaces, or 'places'.[23] In contradistinction, people may also have feelings of fear or anxiety towards other places : Tuan applies the term *topophobia* to describe such a sentiment.[24] In both cases, a psychological relationship to these spaces has emerged, as they acquire an embedded meaning for the people that encounter them. As A. Hopcraft remarked in the 1960s :

Football grounds are not often attractive places in the ornamental sense. Their beauty is the special, environmental kind, appreciable only to people who related the setting to their emotional attachment.[25]

It was, however, John Bale who used Tuan to explain the affective dimensions of sports grounds.[26] Bale's work blends the disciplines of social geography and contemporary cultural theory and draws upon worldwide fieldwork.

Tuan's notions have a strong resonance with football ground development in twentieth century Bengal. Every urban locality in colonial Bengal used to have at least one open space, if not more, to play football, breeding a kind of emotional attachment towards that particular space or ground among people around. This unique attachment of the locals to a sporting space is quite akin to *topophilia*. In the context of gradual contraction of open space and steady disappearance of such football grounds from urban landscape in post-colonial Bengal, this topophilic sensation gave way to a tophobic one. As fewer sporting spaces became available for greater number of localities, a sense of distance and detachment began to grow towards certain playgrounds creating topophobic sensations especially among child, adolescent and young sportsmen. The growing distance between *home/locality* and *open space/playground* has largely moulded the nature of spending leisure of the new generation Bengali middle class youth. Intending or potential players and spectators can hardly get a chance to nourish their pursuit of the game in such a situation. This has a drastic impact especially in the suburbs that used to provide a rich supply of good footballers to the big and small clubs of Calcutta. The dearth in the number of quality Bengali footballers as well as declining spectators' interest in Calcutta football in the late 1980s and the 1990s may be partly attributed to this development. Arguably, the topophilic or topophobic sensations that I have pointed out are reflective of a crisis in Bengali's emotional attachment towards football, once considered to be Bengal's most popular mass spectator sport.

To examine the downswing of football ground development in West Bengal during the last two decades, it is useful to look at the concept of 'gaze' popularized by the French post-structuralist social theorist Michel Foucault. The concept of 'gaze' is taken from Foucault's social history of clinic [27]:

The origins of clinical medicine began with the new examination or 'gaze' that its practitioners brought to bear on the bodies of their patients. Medical experts came to `study their subject' in both senses of the phrases. Throughout the nineteenth century other professions began to gaze upon their subjects as a way of knowing and exercising power. Psychologists, criminologists, prison officers and factory owners utilized the gaze to observe and regulate the bodies of others. Today, the gaze functions most proficiently at the localist and interactional level, as people seek to know the identity, motives and values of each other by gazing upon their face and body.[28]

The disciplinary aspect of 'gaze' is not to be underestimated either: 'Our behaviour is regulated by the gaze of others and by the gaze of our own self-reflection'. [29] Its practical sweep extends into consumer culture and leisure, among tourists, television viewers, high street shoppers and sports spectators. Scholars like John Hargreaves [30] and Richard Giulianotti [31] have explored how the modern stadium accommodates the spectator's *gaze.* Within the football stadium, as Giulianotti has argued, the spectator's 'gaze' is satisfied technically through an unobstructed view and panoramic 'sightlines', permitting the fullest knowledge of events on the park. [32] Moreover, the 'gaze' enjoins the spectator to adopt a 'critical distance' towards football, as found in bourgeois cultural spaces like opera houses and theatres.

An adjacent open space-cum-playground and the locals' 'gaze' towards it - both became instrumental in establishing a social control over the youth in the colonial and immediate post-colonial urban Bengal. Here, the 'gaze' also involved an element of spontaneity. The children's ready and wider access to football grounds not only created a long-term attraction to the game in their adolescence and youth but also bred an emotional attachment that was more spatial than social in character. Since the late 1970s, however, with the gradual disappearance of sporting spaces in urban Bengal, the affective role *of* 'gaze' was sharply diminished. The traditional social control exerted through a 'gaze' of open space sports came to be replaced by a constructed home-knit culture where the critical distance between *home/family* and *open sporting space/young players* no longer remained operational. The confined-to-home leisure pursuits [33] in the absence of sporting space deprived the new generation of experience of and interest in on-field excitement, performance and spectatorship in football. While football fell a victim to this changing relationship of leisure-power-culture,[34] the regular 'gaze' of cricket play at sports grounds hitherto dominated by football and on satellite television in the wake of the game's successful commercialization in the 1990s enthused urban Bengali middle classes to send their boys to cricket coaching centres. The element of parental alia social control thus becomes more constructed than spontaneous. Transition from topophilia to topophobia towards particular sporting spaces as well as the changing affective dimensions of 'gaze' in relation to open space, thus, as I have shown, are useful models to understand the marked decline in the standard and popularity *of* football in post-1970s Bengal.

Conclusion

This essay, as has been streamlined in the Introduction, has intended to make forays into a worthy yet hitherto ignored area *of* social history, viz. sport's interrelationship with environmental issues. Just as the internal physical geography of a sport has had a dependent relationship with local environment and microclimate, the social and economic viability of a sport has shown a long-term dependence on regional environmental stability. Colonial Bengal afforded greater availability and easier reclamation of open space and hence flourishing quantity of football grounds. This, in my opinion, in no insignificant way, contributed to football's intensive social popularization throughout Bengal. Post-colonial West Bengal, however, witnessed gradual entrenchment of open space mostly as a result of refugee influx, population pressure and rapid but somewhat unplanned urbanization. This led to a crisis in the maintenance and development of football ground uniquely articulating power relations at different levels - social, political and economic. The decline in football's standard and popularity in the past two decades can be partly attributed to this environmental imbalance. I have employed the conceptual models of Y. F. Tuan and Michael Foucault to stress this affective dimension of open space and its impact on Bengali social psyche. Arguably, therefore, the intricate relations of open space, sports ground and football play mirror the emotional attachments and the dynamics of social control in the urban life of contemporary Bengal.

Notes and References

I would like to thank Prof. Arun Bandyopadhyay, my supervisor, without whose help, guidance and inspiration this essay could not have been written.

1. For an authoritative discussion of sports geography *see* John Bale, Sports *Geography* (London: Spon, 1989). Also *see* John Bale, *Sport, Space and Society* (London: Routledge, 1992).
2. A path breaking study on this subject has been published recently. Andrew Hignell in his book *Rain Stops Play: Cricketing Climates* (London: Frank Cass, 2003) examines the physical geography of English county cricket, in particular its interrelationship with the local environment and microclimate, and looks ahead to the likely impact the global warming and the altered weather patterns will have on the county game.
3. In this essay, the term *open space* refers to a sizeable plot of plain wasteland lying in between urban agglomerations, which is not specifically used for any civic or commercial purpose.
4. Here 'football ground' does not mean the organized sector of sports ground, i.e., stadiums or enclosed grounds owned and maintained by state authority, sports bodies, maidan clubs or schools and colleges. It rather includes those unorganized pieces of open grounds in the urban area, which are either occupied by local clubs or remain in abeyance without any viable proprietor.
5. 'Urban' Bengal, in the context of present chapter, implies Calcutta and its extended outskirts (presently the Greater Kolkata) as well as its neighbouring suburbs where from Calcutta gets a rich supply of footballers.
6. A useful example on this point is Pradip Sinha, *Calcutta in Urban History* (Calcutta: Firma KLM, 1978). In many such other works, despite recurrent reference to 'maidan', open space or sports ground as such hardly finds a place of worth.
7. For a discussion of football's role as a mass spectator sport in colonial Bengal *see* Kausik Bandyopadhyay, 'Race, Nation and Sport: Footballing Nationalism in Colonial Calcutta', *Soccer and Society,* Vo1. 4, No. 1, pp. 1-19.
8. These suburban towns are situated in the surrounding districts of Calcutta, viz. the two 24 Parganas, Howrah, Hoogly and Nadia.

9. Barefooted Bengali outfit Mohun Bagan Athletic Club created sporting history when it defeated booted European civil and military teams one by one to lift the coveted Indian Football Association (IFA) Shield in 1911. This epic victory has become the most commented upon event in the history of colonial Indian sport. For an understanding of its historical significance *see* Boria Majumdar, 'The Vernacular in Sports History', *Economic and Political Weekly*, Vol. XXXVII, No. 29 (July 20, 2002), pp. 3069-3075; Kausik Bandyopadhyay, '1911 in Retrospect: A Revisionist Perspective on a Famous Indian Sporting Victory' in J.A. Mangan and Boria Majumdar (eds.), *Sport in South Asian Society: Past and Present* (London: Taylor and Francis, 2004); Tony Mason. 'Football on the Maidan : Cultural Imperialism in Calcutta' in J.A. Mangan (ed.), *The Cultural Bond: Sport, Empire, Society* (London: Frank Cass, 1992), pp. 142-153; and Paul Dimeo, 'Football and Politics in Bengal: Colonialism, Nationalism, Communalism' in Paul Dimeo and James Mills (eds.), *Soccer in South Asia: Empire, Nation, Diaspora* (London: Frank Cass, 2001), pp. 57-74.
10. This conflict may have some resonance with the elite conflict or *daladali* in nineteenth century Calcutta. S.N. Mukherjee has elaborated on the nature and forms of this '*daladali*' in his *Calcutta: Myths and History* (Calcutta : Subarnarekha, 1977), pp. 60-85. However, he does not take into consideration the sporting dimensions of this particular conflict in his work. Another interesting study on the bhadralok in late nineteenth century Calcutta with the same lax is John McGuire, *The Making of a Colonial Mind : A Quantitative Study of the Bhadralok in Calcutta, 1857-1885* (Canberra: Australian National University, 1983), especially Chapter- 2, pp. 21-41. For an instructive analysis of the nature of elite conflict in early twentieth century Bengali society *see* J.H. Broomfield, *Elite Conflict in a Plural Society: Twentieth century Bengal* (Los Angeles: University of California Press, 1968), which too sails in the same boat.
11. A series of articles on the need for a stadium published in the IFA Shield souvenirs of the late 1930s bear ample testimony to this fact.
12. For an analysis of football's importance as a cultural nationalist force in colonial Bengal *see* Kausik Bandyopadhyay, 'Football O

Bangalee : Oupanibeshik Banglay Sanskritik Jatiyatabader Prakash', in Gautam Chattopadhyay (*ed.*), *Itihas Anusandhan*-16 (Kolkata : Firma KLM, 2002). *Also see* Bandyopadhyay, 'Race, Nation and Sport'; Mason, 'Football on the Maidan', Dimeo, 'Football and Politics in Bengal'.

13. Paul Dimeo has provided an elaborate analysis of the origin, nature and expression of this rivalry in his article '"Team Loyalty Splits the City into Two" : Football, Ethnicity and Rivalry in Calcutta', in G. Armstrong and R. Giulianotti (eds.), *Fear and Loathing in World Football* (Oxford: Berg, 2001). For a brief introduction to the issue of Ghati-*Bangal* conflict on the *maidan, see* Kausik Bandyopadhyay, 'Sporting Culture and Cultural Nationalism', Occasional Paper, Department of History, North Bengal University (2002), pp. 15-16.

14. Promoters in West Bengal are those builders and building contractors who acquire land legally or illegally and build multistoried residential buildings and commercial complexes on the same.

15. The process of cricket's 'becoming' as the most popular mass spectator sport in India alia Bengal began in 1983 when India lifted the World Cup. It was followed by victory in the Rothmans Cup in 1985 and a series of successes at home in the early 1990s. In the wake of India's international success and the viable projection of cricketing icons like Kapil Dev or Sachin Tendulkar through media, cricket in India experienced successful commercialization and became an integral part of Indian life in the late 1990s. Moreover, the rise of a Bengali cricketing icon in the person of Sourav Ganguly has been an important factor in giving the game a competitive edge over other popular sports in Bengal in recent times.

16. Such footballing violence reached a climax on 16 August 1980 when 16 diehard spectators died in a stampede during a league match between Mohun Bagan and East Bengal at the Eden Gardens, Calcutta.

17. Live telecast of all the matches of World Cup football began in 1986. A few years later Doordarshan started showing recorded matches of Serie A (football league) of Italy. From the early 1990s matches of Euro Cup, Copa America and Premier Leagues of

Spain, England and Latin America began to be telecast either live or recorded through the satellite channels.

18. An excellent treatment of cricket's commercialization in India has been offered in Boria Majumdar, *Twenty Two Yards to Freedom : A Social History of Indian Cricket* (Penguin/Viking, 2004), commissioned by the Board of Cricket Control in India.
19. Both the All India Football Federation (AIFF) as well as the Indian Football Association (IFA) took an inordinately long time to come out of the slumber of amateurism. It was as late as in 1996 that the AIFF organized the first National Football League in India although it is yet to chalk out an effective strategy to make the venture a regular commercial success. It is only very recently that the IFA too have taken some reasonable steps to attract sponsors and commercialize the game in Bengal.
20. While Indian football began its international career as one of the Asian giants in 1947, it has come to a miserable position in world ranking since the 1970s. The Asian Games gold medalists in 1951 and 1961, India is now considered to be a minnow in the Asian football circuit. This slump in international success too has effectively undermined the commercial viability of the game.
21. With the exceptions of L.M. Vijayan and Baichung Bhutia India could hardly produce a viable Indian footballing icon at the national level in the past two decades. Most of the sub-continental football heroes in the 1980s and 1990s from Majid Baksar to Jose Ramirez Barreto were foreign recruits.
22. While local Calcutta league matches between two big clubs still attract at least sixty to seventy thousand spectators at any time, national level Ranji Trophy cricket matches often featuring national cricketers fail to tap in spectators in the four-figure.
23. Y.F. Tuan, *Topophilia* (Englewood Cliffs: Prentice Hall, 1974).
24. Y.F. Tuan, *Landscapes of Fear* (Oxford: Blackwell, 1979).
25 A. Hopcraft, *The Football Man* (London: Simon and Schuster, 1988), p.141.
26. John Bale, *Landscapes of Modem Sport* (Leicester: Leicester University Press, 1994).
27. Michel Foucault, *The Birth of the Clinic* (New York: Vintage, 1975).
28. Richard Giulianotti, *Football : A Sociology of the Global Game* (Cambridge: Polity Press, 1999), p. 80.

29. C. Rojek, *Decentring Leisure* (London: Sage, 1995), p. 61.
30. John Hargreaves, *Sport, Power and Culture: A Social and Historical Analysis of Popular Sports in Britain* (Cambridge: Polity Press, 1986).
31. Giulianotti, *Football,* especially Chapter 4, pp. 66-85.
32. Ibid., p. 80.
33. These pursuits include among others playing video or computer games, watching satellite entertainment channels on sports, music, movie or news through cable TV as well as forced ones such as drawing, recitation, singing, dance or swimming.
34. For an instructive analysis of this triangular relationship in the British context *see* Hargreaves: *Sport, Power and Culture.*

9

Local Self-Government and Sanitation in Colonial Bengal 1920-47

Chittabrata Palit

Wherever the buzzword environment is pronounced it is understood to mean desiccation of forest and the green movement or climatic change and its impact on human settlement.

These are remote ideas of environment. But we are more often concerned with the immediate environment around us and its hazards to public health. The immediate environmental pollution is best combated by improvement of sanitation, through collective effort. The famous demographer Thomas McKeown in his *Rise of Population* explained it by the improvement of nutrition and sanitation from 17th century onwards in Britain. A proper sanitation policy according to him even rendered resort to hospitals redundant. [1] Even Roland Ross wrote fervently for a vigorous sanitation policy in British India at the end of the 19th century for eradication of malaria. His appeal to the Colonial Government of India went in vain and he was asked to keep to clinical work. He had discovered the mosquito cycle of malaria and wanted to destroy the habitat by a vigorous sanitation policy out of Indian revenues. For this he was sent back home. But his discovery made him the winner of Nobel Prize in medicine in 1902.[2]

The importance of sanitation, therefore, cannot be gainsaid. In British India sanitation was a negligible part of public health policy. The 'Indian Medical Service' itself was run by the military department which catered to the needs of the military establishment first and white civilians next. Very little fund was spared for health-care of the Indian people and expenses for the sanitation improvement of the country. The office of a sanitary commissioner was launched in 1864 but its main activities of sewerage control were confined to the urban areas. The rural sector knew no sanitation. Ross was the first to appeal to the government for funds from enormous Indian revenues for controlling mosquito menace in the rural sector to eradicate malaria. The government was in no mood to spend on rural sanitation and Ross had to give up and go back to England. In fact, at the time of Lord Ripon in 1880, the government was harping on the formation of local self-government and self taxation for various rural reforms including sanitation. The ostensible purpose was to create nurseries for politically ambitious Indians but really to get them to tap the various resources at the hinterland of their own expense.[3] The ploy worked and by the Bengal Village Self-government Act of 1919, District Boards and Union Boards were created for rural reconstruction. The government gave some grants in-aid to District Boards but Union Boards were all virtually self-financed by collection of local taxes and cesses. Henceforth, public health and sanitation became their Jurisdiction but government kept a tight control over them through the District Board nominees and the District Magistrates.

Yet this first flush of political power intoxicated the local potentates. They gave a good account of themselves in performing local acts of improvement.

In the first year of its existence in 1920-21 there were many non-starters. But the village committees of the Dhaka district showed 'vitality and energy and were a hopeful augury of public spirit and civil responsibility, The progress report of 1920-21 stated:

"It is contended that the villagers cannot afford to pay taxes for the improvement of their unions and it must be admitted that experience has not yet justified the optimism which held that the villager was shrewd enough to pay if he saw that he was obtaining good value for his money in the shape of improved communications and sanitation".[4]

But the Union Boards received a setback in the hands of the non-co-operators. In Midnapore district there was an organised campaign against the new Union Boards. The Union Boards were held in suspicion as the Act was thought binding on the villages. The report for 1922 lamented that the Union Boards have been represented as merely instruments of new taxation instead of potential agencies for the proper organisation of the village resources.[5]

The Union Boards were withdrawn in the district as a result. The review report of 1922-23 stated that in some unions, there was opposition to the realisation of Union rates. The pay of the chowkidars fell in arrears. It was admitted that the Union Boards were handicapped for want of funds and hence to improve water supply and sanitation.

In Dhaka, the provision of pure water supply received the attention of a large number of Union Boards while others spent money on dispensaries, schools, improvment of village roads, drainage and country justice.

It was estimated that there were 84,981 villages in a province requiring enormous funds for the satisfactory service of water supply in each village. This was impossible for the District Boards and even the government to fund it except through the agency of the Union Boards which must be spread throughout rural Bengal in the interest of sanitation and public health.[6]

The report for 1927-28 praises the efforts of the Union Boards in establishing grants-in-aid Primary schools in which District, Boards had contributed 50% of the fund. In Jessore, a lower primary school was started by the muchis (cobblers) of Kagmari, where children were taught by Hindu teachers of higher caste. 199

tubewells were sunk in Hooghly district and so much was the demand that Union Boards and villagers came out to contribute liberally to the project. The report concludes with satisfaction that the number of Union Boards has increased from 2260 to 3005. The total income of Union Boards had risen to Rs. 56 lakhs of which Rs. 35.2 lakhs were spent on chowkidari establishment leaving larger sums than before for village uplift work like water supply, village roads, dispensaries, even street lighting as under the Howrah Union Boards and courts had become popular.[7] The report for 1928-29 records that Howrah appeared to be the model district of progress in self-government in a single decade, including its own conservancy service. The various Union Boards in other districts sank tubewells, built roads and bridges, set up dispensaries, cut irrigation canals etc.[8]

The years 1929-31 were equally fruitful despite the disruptions due to Civil Disobedience Movement. Useful works like seage clearance (Basudevpur U.B, Howrah), conservancy, night school for labourers exclusively (Sultanpur UB, Birbhum), street lighting (Dormars UB, Rangpur) The Union Boards in Howrah cleared 250 tanks of weeds. The number of Union Boards had reached 4024 and was likely to saturate as 5000, giving a proportion 1 member to 50 voters. Any villagers willing to take up an active part in local affairs would sooner or later be able to take the first step in public life.[9]

The Rowlands Committee recommended the constitution of the Union Boards by elections and no official nomination including that of the president. These should be the exclusive bodies by the villagers. 'We have no doubt that even in the remote areas, there must be many, sound in judgement and well versed in village affairs in whom people have faith and upon whom government could place reliance', the Committee observed.[10] Sir Atul Chatterjee, a member of Bengal Legislature wrote in his tract on Rural Reconstruction (1938), 'Rural reconstruction means in a nutshell making the present a better fellow than what he is at present. All his aspects have to be tackled in a comprehensive manner. His main aspects are fourfold: physical, moral, economic and social'. Chatterjee itemised rural reconstruction as follows : Sanitation, Nutrition Public health, Medical relief, among others.

Wrote Chatterjee, 'There is no question that the conciousness of the rural people can be roused and has been roused in many places. In Bengal, competitions for model villages are taking place. The instance of Sandhipur in Burdwan District may be quoted as an example of what a group of private individual chiefly on voluntary effort, can achieve for the betterment of village sanitation, alleviation of the sufferings from malaria. [11]

This is the beginning of a Panchayati Raj. It was not fully tried out before Independence. The Mehta Committee between 1955-57 sat to plan the Panchayatai Raj. It was tried out in different Places in India since then. In West Bengal Panchayats made a modest but true beginning from 1990. Local decision-making, fund-raising and spending for community developments can solve the problems of sanitation and public health if political faction-fighting does not take the centrestage.[12]

Notes and References

1. Thomas Mckeown, *The Modem Rise of Population*, London, 1976, passim.
2. R.L. Megroz, *Ronald Ross : Discoverer and Creator*, London, 1931.
3. B.B. Misra, District Administration and Rural Development in India. Delhi, 1983, chapter on Local Self-government and C. Palitet al edited Political Economy and Protest in Colonial India, Calcutta 1997. cf. : C. Palit, From the Raj to the Panchayati Raj.
4. Village Self-government Report 1920-21, Calcutta, 1922.
5. Ibid, 1922, Cal., 1923
6. Ibid, 1924, Cal., 1925
7. Ibid, 1927-28, Cal., 1929
8. Ibid, 1928-29, Cal., 1930
9. Ibid, 1929-31, Cal., 1932
10. Report of the Rowland Committee 1944-45, Cal., 1945, Recommendations.

11. Sir Atul Chatterjee, Rural Reconstruction, 1938, Cal., 1938.
12. C. Palit, *op.cit.* Panchayati Raj.

10

Environmental Protection and Sustainable Development : A Peep into the Earth Charter

Narayan Saha

Preamble :

We stand at a critical moment in Earth's history, a time when humanity must choose its future. As the world become increasingly interdependent and fragile, the future at once holds great peril and great promise. To move forward, we must recognize that in the midst of a magnificent diversity of cultures and life forms, we are one human family and one earth community with a common destiny. We must join together to bring forth a sustainable global society founded on respect for nature, universal human rights, economic justice, a culture of peace. Towards this end, it is imperative that we, the people of the earth, declare our responsibility to one another, to the greater community of life, and to future generation.

Earth, Our Home :

Humanity is part of a vast evolving universe. Earth, our home, is alive with a unique community of life. The forces of nature make existence a demanding and uncertain adventure, but the earth has provided the conditions essential to life's evolution. The resilience of the community of life and the well-being of the humanity depend upon preserving a healthy biosphere with all its ecological systems, a rich variety of plants and animals, fertile soil, pure water and clean air. The global environment with its finite resources is a common concern of all peoples. The protection of Earth's vitality, diversity, and beauty is a sacred trust.

The Global Situation :

The dominant patterns of production and consumption are causing environmental devastation, the depletion of resources, and a massive extinction of species. Communities are being undermined. The benefits of development are not shared equitably and the gap between rich and poor is widening. Injustice, poverty, ignorance, and violent conflict are widespread and the cause of great suffering. An unprecedented rise in human population has overburdened ecological and social systems. The very foundation of global security is being threatened. These trends are perilous but not inevitable.

The Challenges Ahead :

The choice is ours: from a global partnership to care for Earth's environment and one another or risk the destruction of ourselves and the diversity of life. Fundamental changes are needed in our values, institutions, and ways of living. We must realize that when basic needs have been met, human development is primarily about being more, not having more. We have the knowledge, science and technology to provide for all and to reduce our impact on the environment. The emergence of a global civil society is creating new opportunities to build a democratic and human world. Our environmental, economic, political, social and spiritual challenges are interconnected and together we can forge inclusive solutions.

Our Responsibility :

To realize these aspirations, we must decide to live with a sense of universal responsibility, identifying ourselves with the whole earth community as well as our local communities. We are at once citizens of different nations and of one world in which the local, regional and global issues are linked. Every one shares responsibility for the present and future well being of the human family and the larger living world. The spirit of human solidarity and kinship with all living and non-living organisms is strengthened when we live with reverence for the mastery of being, gratitude for the gift of life, and humility regarding the human place in nature.

We urgently need a shared vision of basic values to provide our ethical foundation for the emerging world community. Therefore, together in hope, we affirm the following interdependent principle for a sustainable way of life as a common standard by the conduct of all individuals, organizations, business, government, and transitional institutions is to be guided and assessed.

THE PRINCIPLES, COMMITMENTS AND CODE OF CONDUCT AS PER THE EARTH CHARTER:

I. RESPECT AND CARE FOR THE COMMUNITY OF LIFE:

Traditionally geography and history have been concerned with the diversity of life across the surface of this earth. We sought to describe the viability of our earth in ideas, terms, and images of geology, geomorphology, climate, soils, vegetation and the multiplicity of life forms that occurred naturally on the earth. Such study can easily be understood as a facet of respect and care.

1. **Respect for Earth and Life in all its Diversity :**

(a) Recognize that all beings are interdependent and every form of life has value regardless of its worth to human beings.

(b) Affirm faith in the inherent dignity of all human beings and in the intellectual, artistic, ethical and spiritual potential of humanity.

2. **Care for the Community of Life with Understanding, Compassion and Love:**

(a) Accept that with the right to own, manage and use natural resources comes the duty to prevent environmental harm and to protect the rights of people.

(b) Affirm that with increased freedom, knowledge, and power comes increased responsibility to promote the common good.

3. Build Democratic Societies that are Just, Participatory, Sustainable and Peaceful:

(a) Ensure that communities at all levels guarantee human rights and fundamental freedoms and provide everyone an opportunity to realize his or her full potential.

(b) Promote social and economic justice, enabling all to achieve a secure and meaningful livelihood that is environmentally responsible.

4. Secure Earth's Bounty and Beauty for Present and Future Generations :

(a) Recognize that the freedom of action of each generation is qualified by the needs of future generations.

(b) Transmit to future generations values, traditions, and institutions that support the long-term flourishing of earth's human and ecological communities.

In order to fulfill these four broad commitments, it is necessary to cultivate:

II. ECOLOGICAL INTEGRITY:

The study of ecology is a recent fashion and in many ways is a simplified version of geography. In certain cases, the study of ecology is the study of natural systems and geographic locations without considering the impact of people. But in this context, ecology, with its emphasis on the understanding of intricate inter-relationships and mutual benefit of seemingly diverse and unconnected species and system of life, is central to the issues of unsustainable developments.

5. Protect and Restore the Integrity of Earth's Ecological Systems, with Special Concern for Biological Diversity and the Natural Processes that Sustain Life:

(a) Adopt at all levels sustainable development plans and regulations that make environmental conservation and rehabilitation integral to all development initiatives.

(b) Establish and safeguard viable nature and biosphere reserves, including wild lands and marine areas, to protect Earth's life support systems, maintain bio-diversity and preserve our natural heritage.

(c) Promote the recovery of endangered species and ecosystems.

(d) Manage the use of renewable resources such as water, soil, forest products and marine life in ways that do not exceed rates of regeneration and that protect the health of ecosystems.

(e) Manage the extraction and use of non-renewable resources such as minerals and fossil fuels, in ways that minimize depletion and cause no serious environmental damage.

6. Prevent Harm as the Best Method of Environmental Protection and When Knowledge is Limited, Apply a Precautionary Approach:

(a) Take action to avoid the possibility of serious or irreversible environmental harm even when scientific knowledge is incomplete or inclusive.

(b) Place a burden of proof on those who argue that a proposed activity will not cause significant harm, and make the responsible parties liable for environmental harm.

(c) Prevent pollution of any part of the environment and allow no build-up of radio-active, toxic, or hazardous substances.

7. Adopt Patterns of Production, Consumption and Reproduction that Safeguard Earth's Regenerative Capacities, Human Rights and Community well- being:

(a) Reduce, reuse, and recycle the materials used in production and consumption systems, and ensure that residual waste can be assimilated by ecological systems.

(b) Act with restraint and efficiency when using energy, and rely increasingly on renewable energy resources such as solar, wind.

(c) Promote the development, adoption, and equitable transfer of environmentally sound technologies.

(d) Adopt lifestyles that emphasize the quality of life and material sufficiency in a finite world.

8. Advance the Study of Ecological Sustainability and Promote the Open Exchange and wide Application of the Knowledge Acquired.

(a) Support international scientific and technical cooperation on sustainability, with special attention to the needs of developing nations.

(b) Recognize and preserve the traditional knowledge and spiritual wisdom in all cultures that contribute to environmental protection and human well-being.

III. SOCIAL AND ECONOMIC JUSTICE:

Social and economic justice is a twofold concept that has much in common with sustainable development : all derive from a fundamental sense of equity. The keeping of chicken in order to enjoy a supply of fresh eggs is an example of sustainable activity. As long as the chickens are fed and environmental needs are met the chicken will thrive and eggs will be produced. However, if we wish to eat barbecued chicken the view point of chicken will change. In a broader context, the production of chickens for meat may be considered sustainable but the individual chicken would probably prefer to be an egg producer.

9. Eradicate Poverty as an Ethical, Social and Environmental Imperative:

(a) Guarantee the right to water, clean air, food security, uncontaminated soil, shelter and safe sanitation, allocating the national and international resources required.

(b) Empower every human being with the education and resources to secure a sustainable livelihood, and provide social security and safety hats for those who are unable to support themselves.

10. Ensure that Economic Activities and Institutions at all Levels Promote Human Developments in an Equitable and Sustainable Manner.

(a) Enhance the intellectual, financial, technical and social resources of developing nations.

(b) Ensure that all trade supports sustainable resource use, environmental protection and progressive labour standard.

11. **Affirm Gender Equality and Equity as Pre-requisites to Sustainable Development and Ensure Universal Access to Education, Health care, and Economic opportunity.**

12. **Uphold the right of all, without discrimination, to a natural and social environment, supportive of human dignity, bodily health and spiritual well being, with special attention to the rights of indigenous peoples and minorities. Protect and restore outstanding places of cultural and spiritual significance.**

IV. DEMOCRACY, NON-VIOLENCE AND PEACE :

Sustainability depends on stability, stability depends on peace, peace depends on non-violent means of governance and commerce, which, in turn, finally depends on transparency and accountability. The form of government historically most amenable to such needs, and the most inclusive, in basic democracy, which can only function when citizens are educated, well informed, and provided with access to the places and means of decision-making.

13. **Strengthen democratic institutions at all levels and provide transparency and accountability in governance, inclusive of participation in decision-making, and access to justice.**

14. **Integrate into formal education and life-long learning the knowledge, values and skills needed for a sustainable way of life.**

15. **Treat all living beings with respect and consideration.**

(a) Protect wild animals from methods of hunting, trapping and fishing that cause extreme, prolonged, or available suffering.

16. **Promote a culture of tolerance, non-violence and peace. Encourage and support mutual understanding, solidarity, and co-operation among all peoples and within and among nations. Recognize that peace in the wholeness is created**

by right relationship with oneself, other persons, other cultures, other life, earth and the larger whole of which all are a part.

The Way Forward

As never before in history, common destiny beckons us to seek a new beginning. Such renewal is the promise of these Earth Charter principles. To fulfill this promise, we must commit ourselves to adopt and promote the values and objectives of the Charter.

This requires a change of mind and heart. It requires a new sense of global interdependence and universal responsibility. We must imaginatively develop and apply the vision of a sustainable way of life locally, nationally, regionally and globally. Our cultural diversity is a precious heritage and different cultures will find their own distinctive ways to realize the vision. We must deepen and expand the global dialogue that generated the Earth Charter, for, we have much to learn from the on-going collaborative search for truth and wisdom.

Life often involves tensions between important values. This can mean difficult choices. We must find ways to harmonize diversity with unity, the exercise of freedom with the common good, short term objectives with long term goals. Every individual, family, organization and community has a vital role to play. The partnership of government, civil society, and business is essential for effective governance.

In order to build a sustainable community, the nations of the world must renew their commitment to the world organizations, fulfill their obligations under existing international agreements.

Notes and References

1. *Trends in Geography : an Introductory Survey*. Cooke, Ronal U., and James, H. Johnson, 1969, London : Pergamon Press.
2. *Planet Earth in Jeopardy : Environmental Consequences of Nuclear War*, DOHO, Lydia, 1986, John Wiley and Sons.

3. *Progress, co-existence and Intellectual freedom*, Sakharov, Andrei D. 1968, W.W. Norton & Company, Inc.
4. *The Handbook of Ecological Monitoring*, Clarke, Robin, (ed.) 1986. Oxford : Clarendon Press.
5. *Vital Signs 1997 : The Environmental Trends that are shaping our future*, Brown, Lester R., Michael Rennes, and Christopher Flavin, 1997.
6. *Dividing the waters : Food security, Ecosystem, Health and the New Politics of Scarcity Postal*, Sandra, 1996, Washington D.C. Worldwatch Institute.
7. United Nations Environment Programme, 1999, Global Environment Outlook 2000, Nairobi : UNEP.
8. United Nations, 1992. Agenda – 21: The Rio Declaration in Environment and Development, New York, United Nations.
9. National Environment Policy 2004 Ministry of Environment and Forests, Government of India, New Delhi, 21 August, 2004.
10. Environmental Studies : Mukherjee, S & Ghosh, A, Books and allied (P) Ltd, Calcutta, 2001.
11. Study Materials taught and supplied at the Lecture Hall during the Refresher course in Environmental Studies under the auspices of Academic Staff College, Calcutta, 2 November 2004 – 24th November 2004, and support the implementation of Earth Charter principles with an international legally binding instrument on environment and development.

Let ours be a time remembered for the awakening of a new reverence for life, the firm resolve to achieve sustainability, the quickening of the struggle for justice and peace, and the joyful celebration of life.

11

Organic Tea Farming for Maintaining Environment Quality

Sukanya Majumdar

Since of late, resource depletion and environmental abuses have become subjects of much concern among agricultural industries throughout the world. This has occurred due to the changes in agricultural practices with different innovative technologies introduced from time to time to maximize productivity.

It is known that tea is a popular non-alcoholic beverage and refreshing drink having numerous medicinal properties. It is one of the important agro based export oriented crops in India.[1] The first recorded mention of tea in India was in 1780, when a few bushes from Canton were planted in Calcutta, which did not survive for want of culture or due to unfavourable weather or soil conditions. Serious thoughts were given in 1788 for the culture of tea as a commercial proposition in India to replace the monopoly tea trade of China, as until then China was the sole supplier of tea to the Western World. Bihar and Cooch-Bihar were found to be suitable for tea cultivation. It was not however until the annexation of Assam near about 1830, that earnest attention was riveted on this direction. The real progress was recorded in 1834, when Lord William Bentinck, the then Governor General appointed the 'Rea

Committee' to investigate into the possibility of introducing China tea plants into India. Subsequently a government experimental area was opened at Sadiya in Assam with seed from China. Unfortunately the Chinese tea plants which were planted failed to survive with the best of treatment.[2] In the process the genuine trees growing wild in the Hills of Assam near Sibsagar were discovered by Major Bruce. Even between the Dibru and Diking rivers, groups of tea plants were then found suggesting organized planting sometime in the past. It is said that the Singpo tribe in Assam used to prepare a brew like tea and he heard about the tea plants from a Singpo chief. On 8th November 1834 Lieutenant Andrew Charlton, then serving in Sadiya sent seeds and plants of 'Assam Jat' of tea to Calcutta. These plants were confirmed to be tea plants of an indigenous variety by Dr. N. Wallich, Superintendent, Botanical Gardens, Calcutta.

Mr. G.J. Gordon Mackintosh and Company, Calcutta who was sent by Lord William Bentinck, Governor General of India to obtain tea plants from China was called back. But considerable qualities of China tea plants were imported and planted at Chubwa Tea Estate, now a property of Tata Tea Limited and derives its name from 'CHA BOA', meaning 'planted tea'.

With the identification of the tea plants as indigenous trees growing in the forests of Assam, dependence on Chinese variety began to fade from around 1838. Mr. C.A. Bruce, Superintendent of 'Government of Tea forests' found more tea plants in the Manipur hills, hills between Assam and Burma and Tripura. Further expeditions discovered tea plants in Katchu, Negrigram, Nadna, Hingri and Borhat which is now a tea estates of Tata Tea Limited.

In the meanwhile the China variety of tea which were being planted proved successful in the Himalayas and Nilgiris but proved a failure in most parts of Assam except at Chubwa, Dinjoy, Chota Hingri and Jaipur and indigenous variety took over in the plains. Experiments were conducted in South India under the Tea Committee.

Within three years of constitution of the tea committee some samples of tea were made and in the year 1838 the history making shipment was sent to London. The commercial success of the initial plantations attracted a lot of public attention and there was a 'tea mania' leading to the formation of Assam Company, the first tea company in India, by British nationals.[3] Tea was first planted out in Darjeeling areas in 1839, in Sylhet and Cachar in about 1855, in the Terai in 1862 and in the Dooars in 1874. The experiments carried out in South India made little progress until 1883.

The 'tea mania' did not last long as the mushrooming companies became sick due to unwise selection of plots for cultivation. Following the establishment of the Scientific Department of Indian Tea Association at the turn of the century, considerable improvement was done in the field of soil management and pest management. As a result productivity increased by about 15% in less than 10 years. Thus the history of tea industry in India reveals two interesting factors.

(a) That tea was the indigenous plant of India and climatic conditions were favourable for its proper growth and better quality yields.

(b) Proper management of soil and pest increased productivity. Indian tea has since traversed a long distance.

To earn foreign exchange all tea growing countries including India are trying to maximize their production through improved methods of cultivation. In order to keep up to the demand, commercial farming system used like cultivation of tea resort to heavy dressings with chemical fertilizers and other growth stimulators. Nitrogen and phosphorous being key elements for growth of plants are supplied in the form of chemical fertilizers. Other than resulting in higher cost per unit, agricultural produce due to steep escalation in the cost of chemical fertilizer, repeated application of chemical fertilizers resulted, in deterioration of soil health. Excess of nitrate thereof pollutes nearby well, ponds and ground water affecting marine life. Moreover the chemical fertilizer industry contribute considerably to the atmospheric pollution. Among the agro-chemicals the use of fungicides and insecticides like DDT play a vital role in influencing the pest population density.

Pest outbreak occurs in tea also due to human interference in terms of large-scale monoculture with high yielding susceptible tea clones, intensity of shade and over dependence on agrochemical for higher productivity. It is said that one of the major factors responsible for resurgence of mite population in tea is due to high use of copper fungicides for control of Blister blight. The retention of water in soil depends on the texture of the soil and the quantity of organic matter content in it. Huge quantity of chemical fertilizers, pesticides, insecticides, weedicides deteriorates the properties of the soil resulting in gradual fall of productivity and fertility.

In this context I would like to sight an interesting fact relating to the side effect of intensive use of strong chemicals. In the early 50's Malaria was rampant in Brunei and almost 9 out of 10 people were affected. World Health Organisation, under the Malaria Eradication Programme in 1955, undertook intensive spray of a strong insecticide called Dieldrin. Although, the cases of Malaria declined sharply, within a short period incidents of plague appeared and roof of most of the thatched houses started to collapse. This was because the chemical Dieldrin has poisoned the food chain. Most of the mosquitoes were killed but some were merely poisoned and became sluggish and were easy preys for lizards, which in turn were eaten by cats resulting in large-scale mortality of cats. As a result the rats multiplied and plague reappeared. At the same time the other insects, which used to eat the caterpillar larvae in the thatched roof were also poisoned and died. The caterpillars multiplied and ate through the thatch and grass roofs. Thus use of chemicals should be extremely judicious taking care that we do not interfere with the natural feed chains. So the importance of organic farming becomes understood which hopes to gain maximum popularity in the years to come.

According to G.K. Veeresh, who was the Vice Chancellor, University of Agricultural Sciences, Bangalore, Organic farming is best suited under perennial plantation crops which provide proper shade and cover to the soil, which keeps the microbial activity in the soil constant. Mr. S.K. Bhasin, Managing Director, Goodricke

Group of Companies pioneered the organic movement in India has been associated with the oldest and first ever organic tea garden – Mullootar of Darjeeling during 1987. it has been found that organic system of farming has two basic constitutions :

(a) It is a low energy input system.

(b) It is self sustaining, needs no synthetic products in view of the environmental and ecological degradation caused by intensive agriculture, more particularly monoculture.

Organic farming of tea is produced with a commitment to respect biological and ecological process. Organic agriculture perceives nature as more than just the separate, individual elements into which it may be split. The principles of organic tea farming are found in ecology, a science concerned with the inter-relationship of living organisms and their environments. Such farming also covers economic and social aspects of agricultural production, local as well as global.

The aim of organic tea farming is to support and strengthen biological process without recourse to synthetic fertilizers and pesticides and the genetic modification of organisms. Hence this method takes mainly a preventive approach in controlling weeds, pests and diseases through biological process. Tea production and soil fertility is maintained by improving the biomass production, returning the nutrients removed with the harvested leaf by using natural as much as possible local resources and organic by-product, as long as they are pollution free. The estate or farm is a closed system, having limited external inputs only. Thus organic cultivation aims for an ecologically sustainable tea plantation.

The cessation of the use of artificial fertilizer and other agro-chemicals for a period of two to three years is only a start towards the transition to organic farming. Nevertheless, the tea produced during this stage is traded, as transition produce at a reasonably price.

Organically farmed produce is certified as those that are generated from fields practising the correct principles of cultivation by a certification organization, (International Federation of Organic Agricultural Movements). The use of residue analyses is no proof that the tea is grown organically. Inspection is done field visits, checking the organic growing techniques and by a check on farm inputs, field, production and sales.

A crop can qualify as organic when active use is made of various available environment–friendly techniques. This includes evidence of growth of various green manure crops to furnish adequate quantities of compost for organic matter. The practice of green manuring is borrowed from the classical farming that withstood the test of time. It helps the diversity which helps in many ways to develop and interact with micro organism and accumulate nutrients at different strata of soil. Green crop acts as a companion crops and helps each other for better growth, through their inter-relationship. Green manure is behind the growth of leguminous and non-leguminous plants. Various nutrients are available to the soil after it is incorporated. It improves the moisture retention capacity by farming humus. Nitrogen, needed for the growth of plants is released in the process of decomposing green manure which becomes accessible to the roots of the plants.

Incorporation of farmyard manure is an essential requirement for organic farming which leads to organized animal husbandry project.

Organic supplements like neem cake, castor cake is used in place of artificial manures. The soil organic matter on decomposition forms itself some quantity of macro nutrients (N, P, K) and micronutrients (Zn, Cu, Fe, Mn). A natural control of pests and diseases is favoured by regulating biological control methods. Pruning brings about a drastic local curtailment of food supply of pests followed by marked alteration in micro climate. Plucking is a routine measure that has an effect on those pests that causes the crop loss directly feeding on young shoots. Moreover such seedlings are used which are adapted to the local climate, possibly resistant to pest and diseases, having high tolerance to environmental stresses. Weed control is minimized by mulching and soil covers. Some measure of success can also be obtained by use of neem seed oil as an insect / mite repellent. Blister Blight was fought by reducing shade.

Erosion is prevented by planting by terraces on contours, by growing soil covers in empty spaces and by making silt traps in drains. All vacant areas in the field should be filled in with tea and the unsuited areas should be planted with beneficial soil cover.

The adoption of such strategies can be certified as truly "organically farmed". A conversion to organic farming is not a mere shift of farming techniques but rather a shift to an entirely new dynamic and environmentally responsible farming system. Scientific organic farming has been undertaken in North East India and mainly in Darjeeling Hills.

Thus by application of organic farming the fertility of soil could be made improved and aeration much exposed. The method not only prevents soil erosion and also increases capacity of water retention thus helping rejuvenation of the already 'burnt – out' and depleted soil suffered by health injuries in organic farming. Further, recycling of organic wastes generated by public and industries cleans up the environment and its application reduces over-dependence on pesticides, thus reducing the chances of infestation of diseases to tea plants and its effect on consumers. Drinking of tea produced by organic method becomes more healthier and more tastier ensuring increasing demand, better price and good prospect for marketing of the product. Grown under such an ecologically compatible farming concept, tea will become more acceptable to the world population at commercially viable price level in a sustained manner keeping the soil's capacity for production intact without threatening the human and animal existence.

Notes and References

1. The development of Tea Industry in the District of Jalpaiguri (1869 - 1968), B.G. Ghose.
2. Contemporary tea handbook (published by Contemporary Tea Co. Ltd.)

3. Practical aspects of tea culture and manufacture, M. Gupta.
4. Reference also from - West Bengal District Gazetteers, Jalpaiguri, July 1981. Published by - Dr. Barun De.
5. Tea Review Journals (from 1980 – 2002 Dec.), Published by Goodricke Group of Companies and Assam Tea Company.

12

Environmental Crisis and Human Rights : A Historical Perspective

Mahua Sarkar

The present paper seeks to analyze the twin questions of human rights and environment from a historical perspective. The two issues are closely interrelated with the history of human civilizations. The story of human progress is much more than the study of mere political and economic history available in recorded events. The evolution of man since the pre-historic times was the result of a series of physical, mental and sociological adaptations. This adaptation process was determined by the kind of environment and ecology which pre-historic man had to face. The symbiosis between nature and the elements of growth of human societies can be observed from the earliest days of human society.[1]

At the same time, man's control over nature is always conditioned by power and access over material culture. Degradation of environment would bring an end of this earth and it is primarily caused by human activities taking place all around the world. But all humans are not responsible for this degradation, neither all humans have been equally affected for this degradation.

One has to remember in this context that environmental crisis has no definite boundary. It is also an established historical fact that a number of great civilizations disintegrated due to ecological imbalances caused consciously or unconsciously by the people themselves.[2] Many scholars have suggested different explanations regarding the causes of environmental crisis. All these hypothesis are related with questions of balance in nature. The ecologist Paul Ehrlich, in his book 'The Population Explosion' proposes overpopulation as the fundamental cause of the environmental crisis.[3] The environmental economists, Dennis and Donella Meadows, in their report 'The Limits of Growth' identify the economics of growth as the central cause of environmental overexploitation.[4] Robert Attfield, in his book, 'The Ethics of Environmental Concern', identifies the pursuit of progress as the central feature of the modern world-view which has given rise to the environmental crisis.[5] Theodore Roszak,[6] Edward Goldsmith[7] and Rupert Sheldrake[8] argue that the modern scientific method is the source of the distorted relationship between humanity and nature, which has produced the ultimate crisis.

In all these suggestions, the question of human involvement with environment has been always mentioned as an important issue. Indeed, since the European Enlightenment of the 18th Century, the biocentric view of the universe has been transformed into an anthropocentric one.[9] Man and man-controlled Science has become the central theme in the questions of human existence and human progress. Through the deployment of technology, through the social processes of experimentation and observation and through the values of domination and progress, modern science is standing over nature.[10] In other words, the money economy and industrialism, have given rise to a social form, i.e., modernity, which is dedicated to the systematic transformation of human relations with nature. The world is primarily seen as a domain of humans. This approach had also been responsible for a greater knowledge and greater exploitation of the natural resources, causing a steady degradation of the environment.

At the same time, science and technological growth are the two essential prerequisites for modern development. Then, can we say that the twin questions of human rights and environmental crisis are both interrelated and contradictory to each other? Because, as we know, the human rights agenda is also cropping up as an important issue in the modern, contemporary world. Having grown out of liberal traditions of the 18th Century, the language of human rights has become a complex strategy to explicate the demands of various marginal groups. The legal concept of human rights became very important in a specific period of history. In Europe, humanism and human concerns became very important in Western political thought since the 18th Century. It mainly emerged under the umbrella of the philosophical, political and legal values which had gained ground from the Renaissance. The emergence of these values and modern development are inseparable from a long, historical process of economic, social, political and cultural transformation. These ideas are associated with the rise of the middle class, the industrial revolution and the growing unbanisation leading to further overexploitation of natural resources.[11]

The question of human rights is a recent phenomenon, closely related with modernity. But the human rights issues imply that there exists a universal standard of ethical values and human aspirations. [12] The multiple socio-cultural and historical circumstances which shape different societies make this proposition universally untenable. The features of the current international standards of human rights have been primarily conceived, developed and established by the West. They cannot be accepted or implemented globally, unless they are seen to legitimise the perspectives of other cultures as well. A genuine universal model rather than the universalization of a certain culturally specific 'western' model is necessary to solve the contradictions between human rights and environmental issues.[13]

The global politics for the protection of human rights operates through the monitoring of Northern organizations of Violations in the South and lobbying with the Northern governments to pressurise Southern governments to respect the human rights of their own populations.[14] Human rights issues have become an industry in the developed world with organizations such as Amnesty

International and Asia Watch.[15] These concerns are always publicizing human rights abuses in the Third World Countries. The international monitoring has never been a two-way process across the North-South divide.

Moreover, wherever environmental issues are linked with the question of human rights, the matter becomes more complicated. It would be a grave error in understanding that Oriental culture do not have an amity between human rights and understanding of the environment. The conceptions of human rights could be found in most civilizations.[16] If we examine the history of human rights, we find that in all eras and in all regions, men and women, groups and communities have protested against various forms of coercion because of their ideas of justice, human dignity or individual or collective freedom. Much later, in the 20th Century, the Universal Declaration of Human Rights was adopted by the UN General Assembly on 10th December, 1948.[17]

All these earlier and later documents implicate that the problem of human rights is intrinsically bound up with the relations existing between man and his social environment. Today, many historians, economists and sociologists are speaking in terms of a common minimum good, but in practice, the entire development discourse was run by experts, middle class professionals, who stood for the state and through the state for the nation. Politicians and bureaucrats are also guided by the same ideas of self-interest.[18] All this was done in the name of the masses, who entered the picture only as the "somewhat abstract ultimate beneficiary'.[19] One cannot do away with industrialization, but the latter commoditifies nature and treats ecosystems as materials banks, pollution sinks or productivity zones. Even, the enjoyment of nature has become an integral part of the consumer society. The two poles of 'wilderness' and 'civilization', mutually coexist in an internally coherent whole, where the two parts are contradictory. Wilderness reserves or game parks are artificial in their construction of relations between humans and nature, because, indigenous peoples are often excluded from these 'protected' parts of the non-human world which they have respected and preserved and lived off for thousands of years. The radical American environmentalists, proposing the theory of 'Deep ecology', in a militant defence of 'Mother Earth', have attacked all human intrusions or undisturbed wilderness, but the theory has been strongly criticised from a Third World perspective.[20]

In an earlier essay on the tribal situation and environmental crisis in North Bengal, I have shown how the people of the Duars were forced to accommodate themselves with the colonial forest laws of the British Government.[21] In the name of preservation, they were transformed from relatively independent shifting cultivators to settled forest villagers, under the hard supervision of the Forest Department. They could never understand the language of their rights, if at all they were endowed with such things. The laws of the forests were quite distant from the principle of the Rule of Law. The mandate of environmental conservation was given into the hands of a bureaucracy, who had never really bothered about the rights of the tribals.[22]

In the post-independence period, Nehru realised that the rights of the tribals should be restored through the process of indirect interventions.[23] Autonomous tribal councils were created in the North East and tribal majority areas were considered as special zones.[24] In keeping with Nehruvian ideals, a separate Tribal Welfare Department was set up. All tribal areas were divided into special Tribal Multipurpose Blocks for promoting welfare measures like education, public health and income generation activities. But all these programmes were considered in isolation from the larger aims of land use and forest conservation in the post-colonial period.[25] Tribal development could never be compatible with the larger aims of nationalist development.

Naturally therefore, the entire foundation of the Indian environmental movement was based on a demand for wider human rights for the tribals. The early environmentalists protested against Nehru's policy of development as these had led to the displacement of the tribal people. They also argued for a more decentralised model of development. Accordingly, by the 1950s, the advent of neo-liberal globalisation gave rise to 'Community Control' and 'decentralised management' of natural resources. By 1995, fifteen states had begun to implement the Joint Forest Management Programme in their respective areas.[26] But the introduction of this programme had caused the disempowerment of many groups that had spontaneously tried to protect and regenerate forests.

To reduce human interventions, more than 20,000 Protected Areas covering nearly 5% of the earth's land surface have been established in more than 130 countries.[27] In India, the government showed a willingness to prevent rapid decline of wildlife and passed the Wildlife (Protection) Act, 1972. This Act discourages human habitation inside sanctuaries and parks. Forest people are treated as trespassers, their free movement is restricted or stopped. This has led to increasing conflict between the local communities and forest authorities. In practice, many of these areas have a significant human population, living within the forest. They are solely dependent on the Protected Areas for their survival. Bidhan Kanti Das, in his study on *The growth of ethnic groups in forest village of Buxa Tribal Reserve, West Bengal*, suggests that population control of the tribals might be one of the major options to reduce pressure on forest wealth.[28]

But the Census report on the population location quotient, of 2001 shows that a very thin dispersion or very low concentration in the scheduled tribe population exist in as many as 134 districts of India. This kind of dispersion consists of a location quotient ranging from 0.50 and below. A large number of districts in the country have a very low in the context of the population of scheduled tribe population with the country.[29] The lowest range of 3.56-4.50 persons per household in scheduled tribes is recorded in 66 districts of the country.[30]

Madhuresh Kumar, in an appraisal of the National Environment Policy, 2004, comments rightly that the policy itself is controversial and essentially anti-poor.[31] He also argues that a greater emphasis is required at challenging the existing nations as of development, which has already caused a large destruction of the environment. He criticizes the draft of the national policy on tribals, in September 2004, on the ground that the basic principle of the policy is faulty, as it fails to include the scheduled tribes into the mainstream of society.[32] According to a survey report of 2001, only 55.14% of the Toto tribes of North Bengal are earning for their own living.[33]

Problems are however, more complex and complicated. In the backdrop of the present day environmental crisis, the voice of the marginals can be expressed only with an equal economic progress of all. Schemes like a 'Common Minimum Programme' adopted by the UPA can be suggested as one of the probable solutions. The realisation of the Common Minimum Programme would necessarily mean the curtailing of liberalisation and therefore, a confrontation with foreign agencies and domestic vested interests, promoting liberalization is likely to happen. To combat it, the government must have the requisite political will. I hope that such a day is not far away to come.

Notes and References

1. For details see, Bridget Allchin, *Early Man and Environment in South Asia*, 10,000 BC-AD 500 in Richard Grove, V. Damodaran and S. Sangwan (eds.) *Nature and the Orient*, Oxford 1998, pp. 29-50.
2. Biswajit Mukherjee, *Awakening of Environmental Ethics* in B. Mukherjee and Rahul Ray (eds.) *Environmental Awakening*, Chandannagore, May 2005, pp. 10-18. He gives detailed reference to the works of Ferdinand Braudel in this context.
3. Paul R. Ehrlich, *The Population Explosion*, London, 1991.
4. Donella H. Meadows (ed). *The Limits to Growth*, New York, 1972.
5. Robert Att field, *The Ethics of Environmental Concern*, London, 1991.
6. For details, see Theodore Roszak, *Where the Waste Land Ends : Politics and Transcendence in a Post Industrial Society*, London, 1972.
7. Edward Goldsmith, *The Way : An Ecological World View*, London, 1992.

8. *Report* Sheldrake, *The Rebirth of Nature : The Greening of Science and God*, London, 1990.
9. Lynn White, *The Historical Roots of Our Ecologic Crisis*, London, 1967.
10. V. T. Thamilmaran, *Human Rights in Third World Perspective*, New Delhi, 1990, Ch. I, pp. 25-65.
11. Ibid.
12. Veena Ponacha, *Gender Within the Human Rights Discourse*, RCWS, Mumbai, 1995, Introduction.
13. *Ibid.*
14. *Ibid.*
15. *Ibid.*
16. V. T. Thamilmaran, *op.cit.*, pp. 25-65.
17. V. T. Thamilmaran, *op.cit.*, pp. 25-65.
18. Sabyasachi Chatterjee, *An Environmental Movement Against the Greater Common Goods*, in B. Mukherjee and Rahul Ray (eds). *op.cit.*, p. 180.
19. Deepak Kumar, *Science and Society in Colonial India : Exploring an Agenda, Proceedings of the Indian History Congress : Diamond Jubilee Session*, Calcutta, 1999, p. 446, in S. Bhattacharyya (ed)., *Mountains and Forests.*
20. S. Biswas, *A Tale of Two Worlds, in Indian History*, Kolkata, 2004, pp. 261-274.
21. Mahua Sarkar, *Colonial Power and Tribal Space : The Environmental Crisis in North Bengal*, in R. Chakrabarti (ed.) Space and Power in History, Penman, 2001, pp. 107-118.
22. For a brief history of the Indian Environmental Movement, Ramchandra Guha and Juan M. Alier, (eds.) Varieties of Environmentalism, Essays North and South, OUP; 1998, pp. 4-6.
23. Jawaharlal Nehru, *Approach to the Tribes* in **Jawaharlal Nehru's Speeches, 1953-57**, pp. 458-461. For a detailed analysis, see A. Prasad *The Baiga, Local Economy and Survival in Central Provinces* in Studies in History, 1998.
24. *Ibid.*
25. Mark Poffenberger and Betsy Megean (eds), *Village Voices : Forest Choices, Joint Forest Management in India*, Delhi, 1996, Introduction.
26. Ibid.

27. Bidhan Kanti Das, *Growth of Ethnic Groups in Forest Villages of Buxa Tiger Reserve, West Bengal*, in *The Indian Forester*, Vol. 131, No. 4, April 2005, pp. 504-518.
28. Ibid.
29. Census of India, 2001, p. 29.
30. Census of India, 2001, p. 41.
31. Madhuresh Kumar, *National Environment Policy, 2004 : An Appraisal*, in *Policies and Practices*, Mahanirban, Calcutta Research Group, Vol. 6, March 2005, pp. 50-78.
32. Ibid, pp. 75-78.
33. Bulletin of the Cultural Research Institute, Government of West Bengal, 2002, Vol. 21, Special Issue, p. 47.
34. For details, *Social Scientist* (New Delhi), Vol. 32; Nos. 7-8, July-August 2004, pp. 374-375. Editorial. Also Amiya Kumar Bagchi, *The Common Minimum Programme. The finances of the State Government and the urgent tasks of repair and reconstruction* in the same volume.

13

Colonial Exploitation of Indian Forestry

Rupak Ghoshal

During the colonial period Indian forest and animal world were destroyed and exploited brutally by the British rulers and by the British people who came to India. I want to draw a picture about it. But one thing we have to admit that after Independence our Indian government could not take any strong measure to protect our floral and faunal world. In colonial India the British rulers made many laws to protect it but exploited it at the same time.[1]

Here is the outline of the context which made the Nilgiri Game and Fish Preservation Act, 1879 and the argument is the shikar or game-hunting by the British to affirm the difference between its 'superior' self and the inferiorized 'native' the other.[2] From the 1820s onwards, game-hunting in the Nilgiri hills became a favourite pastime among its residents and the representatives of the British Government in India helped to organise it steadily.[3] Like this the Nilgiri hills became the fertile grounds for the hunting of tigers, bisons, jackals, sambhur, spotted deer and so on for the British visitors.[4]

The British were doing pig-sticking in their own country and after coming to India, they at first became familiar with the mystic and dense jungles of India full of such numerous variety of animals that they never seen before. The cause behind this kind of extensive hunting culture was just pleasure and nurturing a distinct masculine physical culture.[5] They were even shooting the peacock, jungle fowl, rabbits etc., carelessly and brutally.[6] The British hunters were enjoying game meat almost everyday and they were much more interested in acquiring trophies.[7] They even ate the flesh of bear with great delight.[8]

The hunting area was surveyed and an precise map was prepared to make a new comer familiar with this country.[9] The Nilgiri Game and Fish Preservation Act of 1879 became more stringent with time but the colonial Government encouraged the hunters with giving the permission of license for hunting. This license was not affordable for any Indians and the Europeans used it and a list of animals the hunters could not hunt which was like this – two sambhar stags, two spotted deer stags, six jungle sheeps, one ibex, three antelopes and one bison.[10] So we can see easily that the British destroyed our animal kingdom instead of protecting it. This incident of Nilgiri hills is only a very little portion of massive destruction of animal resources of India which was done by the British.

Now we would like to cast a glance on the forest policy of the colonial rulers. An important recent study of colonial forestry in India, for example, devotes no more than three pages to forest science.[11] Even it ignores continental traditions and makes no attempt to forest management in the empire in the light of ethos of German and French forestry.[12] The emergence of the continental forestry tradition led also to the creation of a technological and often technocratic elite with a monopoly over decision-making on forest use.[13]

Dietrich Brandis appointed Inspector-General of Forests of India and during 1863-65 and 1868-70 he toured extensively and established forest management in northern India. He also arranged for the continental training of prospective Indian foresters and in 1878 he established the Dehra Dun school for Indian foresters.[14] Like the foresters of Germany and France, Brandis argued that forests offered direct and indirect benefits. He also said that forests had an environmental utility. Brandis stated that the objectives of forest management involved ensuring effective protection of forests against natural and human destruction.[15]

What Brandis's method achieved was to enable the forester to ignore these 'arbitrary details of nature' and concentrate on producing approximations of the extent of teak, the predominant commercial species. Like German forestry it thus leveled across the inherent diversity of forests and produced an efficient scheme to exploit them. It also led eventually to the transformation of these forests into commercially marketable monocultures. Brandis applied his method in other parts of India where he worked, such as the North East provinces and Oudh from where it spread to various parts of the equatorial tropics.[16]

Now we look at the impact of Continental forestry tradition on the British Empire and the agendas and ideologies of natural resource management implicit in colonial forestry in the period 1850-1900. It has been argued that as a framework of resource management, there was nothing particularly distinctive about forestry as practised in the colonial context. There was a strong commitment to building a regime of natural resource management that could cater efficiently to the industrial needs of the nation. An attitude to nature, the agenda of British colonial forestry was unambiguously utilitarian, conservationist as opposed to preservationist.[17]

The British colonial forestry in the nineteenth century inherited the Continental forestry attitude to other forest resource users, especially agricultural populations. Forests in India, in the second half of the nineteenth century, had a clear bias against such communities, whom they viewed as ignorant, environmentally profligate and wasteful. In seeking to objectively define the forest for the purposes of scientific management, they therefore devised a system of curtailing traditional rights, which in time developed into a sub-discipline of forestry-forest law. Thus an authoritarian technics in the realm of forests began.[18]

The local populations were scientifically and technologically backward – this was the critical attitude of the colonial foresters and for this local population's claims were illegitimate. Michael Adas has argued that machines were used by European colonizers 'as the measure of men'.[19] It is tempting to apply such an analysis to the case of British colonial forestry.

European expansion brought with it a new level of environment destruction. From the mid-eighteenth century onwards colonial commerce was characterized primarily by the export of raw materials. This could only become profitable in combination with territorial control of the productive areas. In this context the plantation of cash crops was only worthwhile on a large scale, with the aim of achieving and maintaining low prices for the raw materials produced. This was followed by the East India Company in India. The Indian peasants in the Doab obliged to sow ever more of their land with 'more valuable crops' which commanded higher prices than foodcrops both on local and world markets. The dependence of the agrarian economy had been achieved by more or less subtle means; questions regarding the condition of the people, the soil, the flora and fauna of the intensive agricultural system did not at first concern the East India Company.[20]

There was no agriculture in the central low lands in 1800 except Mainpuri, Etah, Etawah and Aligarh and the ecological balance was completely dependent on dense dhak tree jungle.[21] But the deforestation began. Before 1820 there was thick dhak jungle in the northern part of Aligarh district and in Buland-shahar district. Most of this jungle was cut down in the following three decades.[22] During 1840, over half of the district cultivated, no more expansion was needed. The rest of the dhak jungle disappeared in the second half of the nineteenth century. One of the contemporary observer reported that the belt of jungle upto 3 miles wide disappeared in the ten years following British arrival there.[23]

Around 1850 there was no remaining forest in the area beyond a small patch south of Bharatpur.[24] In Mainpuri, Etah and Etawah, during 1850 and by the end of the nineteenth century every tree had been destroyed.[25] The dhak jungle in the Doab have been chopped down in the first half of the nineteenth century, because Kanpur and Allahabad became cotton centres.[26] Large areas of jungle were destroyed to prevent criminal activities and for agrarian expansion.[27] The estates of rebellious zamindars had been forcibly dissolved and auctioned. When there was no buyer for the above estates, local British officers were ordered to chop down and sell the trees.[28] For manufacturing bricks no longer exactly calculable proportion of the felled timber was used for fuel.[29]

The most prominent causes of forest degradation include excessive removal of timber, fuel and forest products even in the early nineteenth century.[30] Sainthill Eardley-Wilmot, who entered the Indian Forest Service in 1873 and retired as Inspector-General in 1908, described the impact of forest degradation.[31]

Sal is a north Indian timber tree which is so common, strong and wrought. This species was overexploited by nineteenth century timber contractors charged with providing railway ties and constructional materials.[32] Sal has also been subjected to sustained long-term exploitation for local construction use, and as a source of firewood. Its history demonstrates the importance of interactions between environmental and historical factors in the development of modern Indian landscape.[33]

In the late eighteenth century the range of sal was still considerably greater than that shown in Brandis's 1883 map. The forest comprising the northern sal tract extended considerably further south of the Himalayan foothills, particularly in what are now West Bengal and Bangladesh, in military maps prepared by Rennell.[34] The primary factor responsible for the reduction in the range of sal during the century elapsing between the preparation of Rennell's and Brandis' maps was conversion of forest to agricultural land, particularly along the frontier between settled Gangetic plain districts and the Terai forests.[35] For example, rapid population growth in eastern Uttar Pradesh during the early nineteenth century is known to have driven expansion of the area occupied by agricultural land, which 'rapidly extended' invading and sweeping away the forests bordering the areas already occupied.[36] Sal was in demand during the British colonial period for heavy construction (piles, beams, planking, bridge railings) as well as for cart bodies, gun carriages, residential beam and doorposts.[37]

After the war of 1857 the East India Company was replaced by the British crown as the colonial Government of northern India. The new administration invested massively in railway development.[38] An enormous volume of sleepers (railroad ties) was required for this new construction. Each mile of newly laid track required 1760 sleepers.[39] Broad-gauge sleepers were over 3 meters long, so a single felled tree of average dimensions yielded only three to five sleepers of this size.[40] The volume of a metro-gauge sleeper is half the volume of the broad-gauge sleeper,[41] so a typical felled tree would be convertible to six to ten sleepers of that size.

Few timber species in India were sufficiently strong, tough and resistant to termites and fungal decay to be used as railway sleepers, and only three species meeting these criteria were available in large quantities; sal and deodar in northern India, and teak in the south. Accessible forests of all three species were ruthlessly over felled by zealous contractors responding to the unprecedented demand for timber during the first decade of railway expansion.[42]

The Britishers have taken away precious woods from our land to a massive extent to use those for the manufacture of fashionable furnitures and the making of the ball-dance floors.[43] The focus of this article is on Nilgiri hills, some parts of south and north India, but the analysis is more or less applicable to the rest of the country under the colonial rule. However, it would not be irrelevant to mention the fact that the post-colonial era has also witnessed the ruthless exploitation of the forestry that may even be comparable to the brutality of the colonizers. In spite of the world wide campaign against environmental disaster, most of the people belonging to the intelligentia and the academic world are awkwardly indifferent to the crisis in the real life situations. They should keep in mind that environmentalism is not an abstraction; and the existing ecological scenario demands genuine commitment, determination and hardwork from the so-called intellectuals. The idea of free market and the growth model of the neo-liberalist policies have also their far reaching contribution to the ecological disaster and India is not immune to the impacts of these policies. The 'mock "laissez-faie" attitude of the upholders of financial liberalization', in the words of William K. Tabb, 'extends to the environment and to the acceleration of global warming and other destructive policies fostered by the greed of transnational corporations'.[44]

Bibliography

1. Richard H. Grove, *The Green Imperialism*, Oxford Press and Madhav Gadgil, Ramachandra Guha, *This Fissured Land*, Oxford Press.
2. Richard H. Grove, Vinita Damodaran and Satpal Sangwan (ed.) *Nature and the Orient, The Environmental History of South and Southeast Asia*, Oxford University Press, 2000, p. 273.
3. W. Francis, Madras District Gazetteers : *The Nilgiris*, Madras, 1908, pp. 35-36, (Quoted from Richard H. Grove, Vinita Damodaran and Satpal Sangwan (edited) – *Nature and the Orient, The Environmental History of South and Southeast Asia*, Oxford University Press, 2000, p. 273.)
4. Big Bore, *Guide to Shikar on the Nilgiris*, Madras, 1924, xvii, (Quoted from *Nature and the Orient,* Oxford University Press.)
5. Capt. Walter Campbell, *The Old Forest Ranger*, London, 1844, p. 25-4, 49 and Killdeer, *Timely Hints to Amateur Shikaries*, Madras, 1909, p. 4. (Quoted from *Nature and the Orient,* Oxford University Press.)
6. Campbell, *The Old Forest Ranger*, p. 1. (Quoted from *Nature and the Orient,* Oxford University Press.)
7. SIO Apr., 1877 (Quoted from *Nature and the Orient,* Oxford University Press.)
8. Big Bore, *Guide to Shikar*, p. 101. (Quoted from *Nature and the Orient,* Oxford University Press.)

9. Illustrated Guide to the Nilgiris, p. 60. (Quoted from *Nature and the Orient,* Oxford University Press.)
10. SIO, 28 May, 1879; Big Bore, *Guide to Shikar*, p. 128. (Quoted from *Nature and the Orient,* Oxford University Press.)
11. R. Guha, *The Agenda of Scientific Forestry* in *The Unquiet Woods: Ecological Change and Peasant Resistance in the Himalayas*, Delhi, 1989, pp. 59-62.
12. Despite fleeting reference to the standard texts on continental forest history, such as Fernow, *A Brief History of Forestry and* Heske, *German Forestry*, there has been no attempt, whatsoever, to draw on the historical literature on continental Forestry. (Quoted from *Nature and the Orient,* Oxford University Press.)
13. Richard H. Grove, Vinita Damodaran and Satpal Sangwan (ed.) *Nature and the Orient - The Environmental History of South and Southeast Asia*, Oxford University Press.
14. Dictionary of National Biography, 1901-17, pp. 217-18; A. Rawat, *Brandis : The Father of Organised Forestry in India*, in A. Rawat (ed.), *Indian Forestry : A Perspective*, New Delhi, 1993. (Quoted from *Nature and the Orient,* Oxford University Press.)
15. D. Brandis, *Progress of Forestry in India*, Transactions of the Scottish Agricultural Society, 1994, pp. 15-16. (Quoted from *Nature and the Orient,* Oxford University Press.)
16. Rawat, *Brandis*, pp. 86-89; Dawkins, *Sylviculture in the Tropical Rain Forest*, p. 33. (Quoted from *Nature and the Orient,* Oxford University Press.)
17. Richard H. Grove, Vinita Damodaran and Satpal Sangwan (ed.), *Nature and the Orient - The Environmental History of South and Southeast Asia*, Oxford University Press.
18. L. Mumford, *Technics and Civilization*, London, 1934.
19. M. Adas, *Machines as the Measure of Men : Science, Technology and Ideologies of Western Dominance*, Ithaca, 1989. (Quoted from *Nature and the Orient,* Oxford University Press.)
20. Richard H. Grove, Vinita Damodaran and Satpal Sangwan (ed.), *Nature and the Orient - The Environmental History of South and Southeast Asia*, Oxford University Press.
21. Ibid.
22. Home Misc. Series, 776, Appendix to Lord Moria's Minute, 2 Oct., 1815, Judicial Farruckabad, no. 22, in no. 27, in no. 2, para 9. (Quoted from *Nature and the Orient,* Oxford University Press.)

23. W.H. Sleeman, *Rambles and Recollections*, London, 1844, Vol. 1, p. 75.
24. *From Sepoy to Subedar, seeing the life and adventure of Subedar Sita Ram*, James Lunt (ed.), London, 1970, p. 24. (Quoted from *Nature and the Orient,* Oxford University Press.)
25. DGUP, Vol. 10, Mainpuri, p. 23; and report on the Settlement of the Mainpuri District, Allahabad, 1875, p. 10. (Quoted from *Nature and the Orient,* Oxford University Press.)
26. DUGP, Vol. 19, Cawnpore, Allahabad, 1909, pp. 3, 13-14. (Quoted from *Nature and the Orient,* Oxford University Press.)
27. Report on the Settlement of the Mainpuri District, p. 10; Home Misc. Series, p. 776, Appendix to Lord Moira's Minute, Judicial Farruckabad, no. 22, in no. 2, pt. 3, para 5. (Quoted from *Nature and the Orient,* Oxford University Press.)
28. J. Donithorm, *Coll. Of Furruckabad to Board Comms.*, Farruckabad, 16 Oct., 1818, Furruckabad, p. 23, Oct. 1818, BRP, CCD, 1818, IOL (93/37), No. 14, Para 4. (Quoted from *Nature and the Orient,* Oxford University Press.)
29. A.F. Corbett, *The Climate and Resources of Upper India*, London, 1874, pp. 65-66. (Quoted from *Nature and the Orient,* Oxford University Press.)
30. Reginald Heber, *Narrative of a Journey through the Upper provinces of India, from Calcutta to Bombay*, 1824-25 (With Notes upon Ceylon), An Account of a journey to Madras and the Southern Provinces, 1826, and Letters written in India, 2 Vols., Lea Philadelphia, 1829, Vol. 1, p. 406. (Quoted from *Nature and the Orient,* Oxford University Press.)
31. S. Eardley Wilmot, *Forest Life and Sport in India*, London, 1910, p. 9. (Quoted from *Nature and the Orient,* Oxford University Press.)
32. Richard H. Grove, Vinita Damodaran and Satpal Sangwan (ed.), *Nature and the Orient - The Environmental History of South and Southeast Asia*, Oxford University Press, p. 425.
33. Ibid, p. 425.
34. J. Rennell, *A Bengal Atlas Containing Maps of the Theater of War and commerce on that side of Hindustan*, London, 1780.
35. Richard H. Grove, Vinita Damodaran and Satpal Sangwan (ed.), *Nature and the Orient - The Environmental History of South and Southeast Asia*, Oxford University Press, p. 429.

36. E.P. Stebbling, *The Forests of India*, 3 Vols., London, 1922, 1923, 1926, Vol. 1, p. 196. (Quoted from *Nature and the Orient,* Oxford University Press.)
37. Richard H. Grove, Vinita Damodaran and Satpal Sangwan (ed.), *Nature and the Orient - The Environmental History of South and Southeast Asia*, Oxford University Press, p. 433.
38. R.P. Tucker, *The Forests of the Western Himalayas : The Legacy of British Colonial Administration*, Journal of Forest History, 26 (1982), pp. 112-123. (Quoted from *Nature and the Orient,* Oxford University Press.)
39. E. Davidson, *The Railways of India with an account of Their Rise, Progress and Construction*, written with the Aid of the Records of the India Office, London, 1868. (Quoted from *Nature and the Orient,* Oxford University Press.)
40. Ibid.
41. R.G. Marriott, *Sleeper Woods and Sleeper Supply in India*, Emp. For. Jrnl. 7 (1928), pp. 76-83. (Quoted from *Nature and the Orient,* Oxford University Press.)
42. Richard H. Grove, Vinita Damodaran and Satpal Sangwan (ed.), *Nature and the Orient - The Environmental History of South and Southeast Asia*, Oxford University Press, p. 437.
43. Madhav Gadgil, Ramachandra Guha, *This Fissured Land*, Oxford University Press.
44. Analytical Monthly Review, November 2003, Vol. 1, No. 8, Cornerstone Publications, Kharagpur, Midnapur, W.B., India.

14

Globalization and the Indian Cosmetic Industry

Chandrakala Dutta (Roychowdhury)

Notions of beautification of the Indian woman and the use of cosmetics are of long standing tradition in this country. From the ancient period as in the Indus Valley times we find references to the use of collyrium, lipstick and hair oil by both men and women. The use of bangles for ornamentation on the bronze figure of the dancing girl of the Indus Valley civilization is also known. Explicit references to the 'Shringar', the beautification and the ornamentation of the beautiful Vasantsena have also been found in Sudraka's 'Mrichcha Katika' or the Little Clay Cart in early century A.D. Similarly Vatsyayana's 'Kamasutra' is also replete with notions of beauty and dressing up. This tradition continued even in the Mughal period when there are references to the export of India-made perfumes to neighbouring countries, particularly the west. Even all the classical dance forms in India are full of references to the 'Shringar Rasa'.

So beautification of the Indian woman is not so much a post colonial notion as the present generation of youth may be led to believe. But what is new is that with colonization, the concept of beautification changed in the European eyes. All kinds of cosmetics manufactured in the West gradually captured the mind of the Indian woman. In this way India with her large population became a major market for the Western products.

In the post-1947 and more so in the post-Cold war era, with the world becoming increasingly unipolar and the USA becoming the centre of global politics, the concept of beauty is fast changing. Fresh notions of beauty, importations from the West have endangered the environment of the Orient. The international beauty pageants have helped in the globalization of the cosmetic industry through large scale advertising of the products of the West, adorned by, in recent times, mostly Asian mannequins. This has had a wide-spread and far-reaching effect as far as the masses are concerned and Companies like Avon, Revlon, L'Oreal, Oriflame, Maybelline and Synergie have found a ready market with Indians who may well afford them.

The demand for these products is virtually on the rise as the need to look presentable if not 'beautiful' among the youth of both sexes and more so the working population is becoming discernible. Although concepts of beatification and ornamentation were there, there had not been such a tremendous diversification in the cosmetic industry as is lately happening. This is again perhaps related to the fast lives that we are leading and also to the fact that women in large numbers are going to work, thereby in the face of our daily brush with nature the need to take care of one's looks and health. Also because of the increasing purchasing power among a large section of the populace. Previously Indian brands like Nivea, and Lakme, a shampoo, hair oil or cold cream would be sufficient for our mother's use. But now shampoos for all hair types, moisturizers, sun-screen lotions, perfumes, creams suited to different skin types are marketed in India through the Multinational Companies like Avon, Revlon, Oriflame etc. What is interesting is that these companies like Avon and Oriflame through their retailers/ agents have managed to rope in even the middle class Indian housewife to sell these commodities in return of a not so meagre income.

According to a market survey conducted in one of the more renowned cosmetic stores of Gariahat, Lakme once marketed by

TATA has been taken over by Hindusthan Lever, the Indian brand name of Lever Brothers of the USA who have their outpost in other Asian countries such as Pakistan[1]. Products like Pantene were produced by the foreign Multinational Companies in India but now because it is profitable to manufacture the same outside India, for example, in Malaysia, manufacturing units in India have been shut down.

Moreover these foreign cosmetic companies have a very dynamic marketing strategy. There is daily monitoring of the quantum of sales of these shops. Efforts are also made towards push-sales through the agents. The annual turnover of these foreign companies is immense and the Indian companies stand nowhere in the scenario as far as profits are concerned.

Apart from this politics that is going around in the field of cosmeticology, there is another dimension to the globalization of the cosmetic industry. Indigenous companies like Biotique, Lotus, Shehnaz herbal, the Himalaya Drug Company have also made serious inroads into the national as well as the international cosmetic scenario. But the quantum of the total market share that they have been able to corner is not yet substantial when compared to the foreign companies. Not only that Oriental products are studied by the West where indigenous traders play second fiddle. Thus as over basmati India has lost her patent, similarly Indian monopoly on sandalwood camphor, turmeric, basil, honey has been destroyed or is on the verge of being so. If this trend continues then maximum resources from the South will continue to go to the technology rich nations of the North like America.

The need of the hour, therefore, is to tap the steadily increasing global demand for herbal products to make India self reliant in the manufacture of cosmetics as well. Herbs are useful as drugs and remedies to cure and mitigate not only diseases but also as dietary supplements and in overall health care such as in hygienic and cosmetics of the world populace.

It is to be noted that biodiversity countries with the presence of over 45,000 different plant species, India's diversity is due to the presence of 16 different agro-climatic zones, 10 vegetation zones, 25 biotic provinces, 426 biomes (habitats of specific species). Herbal products are worthy of attention but may suffer from the lack of one or more forces to drive them into consumer consciousness and benefit. Thus India has herbs like aswagandha which is an anti-stress product, amla which acts as an antioxidant herb for the heart, shilajit which facilitates the circulation of the bio-active constituents, vasanti which acts as an anti-depressant and mood elevator and which has benefitted millions of people in Germany over the last 10 years.

In view of the large biogenetic resources in our country,[2] the proper utilization of biological resources, the need to patent the products or processes is very essential in the new Intellectual Property Rights' (IPR) regime. Previously it was held that the natural world was the "common heritage of mankind" but this has been replaced by the principle that nation states have sovereign rights over their own biological resources. This it is believed would protect the South from the industrialized nations of the North and that the Convention of Biological Diversity (CBD) signed on the 29th December 1993 between the developed and developing countries with its objective of the conservation of biological diversity, its sustainable use and benefit sharing by access to resources and transfer of technology is a move made towards it.[3]

India can stop the exploitation of her natural resources, the politics of globalization centering around the cosmetic industry and infiltration of the West in our daily lifestyle and endangering of the environment of the Orient by becoming a large and steady market for products of the Occident by developing indigenous enterprise. This can be done through credible research involving chemical, biological and clinical trials, high quality manufacturing and honest claims in marketing are prerequisites to develop herbal based cosmetics on a global basis.

Notes and References

1. *Market Survey in a Cosmetic Store*, Bose & Sons., Gariahat.

2. Science Journal, *Science & Culture*, Vol. 68, Indian Science News Association Special Issue on Pharmaceutics, Jan.-Apr. 2002, Published. from Kolkata.
3. Science Journal, *Science & Culture*, Vol. 68, Indian Science News Association Special Issue on Pharmaceutics, Jan.-Apr. 2002, Published from Kolkata.

Index